Job English
BUSINESS PIONEER

Jooyoung Yoon

Contents

Job

CHAPTER 01 Human Resources — 5
Hiring an Employee | Interview with a Training Manager

CHAPTER 02 Finance & Accounting — 11
Reporting First Half Profits | Confirming Settlement of Accounts

CHAPTER 03 Sales — 17
Domestic Sales | International Sales

CHAPTER 04 Advertising & Marketing — 23
Advertising Concept | Marketing Target & Method

CHAPTER 05 Production & Manufacturing — 29
Talking About Output | Apologizing for Delay

CHAPTER 06 Quality Control — 35
Talking About Defect Rate | Taking About the Quality

CHAPTER 07 Materials — 41
Purchasing Materials | Selling Materials

CHAPTER 08 Research & Development — 47
Market Research | Checking Development Progress

CHAPTER 09 Technical Issues — 53
Technical Contact | Technical Support

CHAPTER 10 REVIEW — 59

Topic

CHAPTER 11	Company	63
	Introducing Your Company | Talking about Company System	
CHAPTER 12	Careers & Jobs	69
	Talking About Your Responsibilities | Current Project	
CHAPTER 13	Colleagues	75
	Talking with a New Employee | Introducing a Colleague	
CHAPTER 14	Products	81
	Introducing a Product | Answering to Inquiry of a Product	
CHAPTER 15	Conflicts	87
	Dealing with Technical Inquiry | Suggesting How to Overcome Conflict	
CHAPTER 16	Collaboration & Cooperation	93
	Distributing Responsibilities | Requesting for Cooperation	
CHAPTER 17	Culture	99
	Company Dress Code | Discussing a Business Motto	
CHAPTER 18	Business Communication	105
	Videoconferencing | In-company Bulletin Boards	
CHAPTER 19	Achievement	111
	Recognition | Getting a Promotion	
CHAPTER 20	REVIEW	117
ANSWER KEY		121

BUSINESS
PIONEER

Section 1 Job

CHAPTER 01

Human Resources

WARM UP

1. How does your company hire new employees? What is the hiring process like?

2. What would you expect an HR manager to do? Would you like to work in HR? Why or why not?

3. What kind of staff training have you had? What kind of training would you like to have?

Unit 01

HiEnglish

Hiring an Employee

STEP 1 PREPARATION

The HR director, Jeff, and the general manager, Sophia, are meeting to discuss candidates for an open job position. Listen to the conversation and answer the following questions.

1. Which candidate do they prefer and why?

2. What are the relative strengths of Diane over Andrew?

3. Why is Jeff hesitating to hire Diane at the moment?

STEP 2 LISTENING

Listen to the conversation again and fill in as many blanks as you can.

Jeff	So after _____ _____ _____ _____ _____, two candidates, Diane and Andrew really stand out.
Sophia	I agree. Well, between Diane and Andrew, _____ _____ _____ _____ the better candidate?
Jeff	It's a tough one. The both are very qualified.
Sophia	Right. Well, what we really need is a smart person who will _____ _____ _____ our organization.
Jeff	Yes, Diane is probably _____ _____ _____ _____. I think her dynamic style aligns well with our organizational culture.
Sophia	Then, what's _____ _____ _____?
Jeff	Well, the main issue I'm worried about is compensation. Her salary history suggests she wants something _____ _____ _____ _____ of our range.
Sophia	Well, let's give her an offer and see how she reacts. _____ _____ _____ we can keep Andrew on the back burner.
Jeff	_____ _____ what I was thinking.

STEP 3 LANGUAGE DEVELOPMENT

Complete the sentences with the right expressions from the box below.

① candidate
② stand out
③ fit well with
④ hold back
⑤ compensation
⑥ in the meantime
⑦ on the back burner
⑧ that's exactly

1. Both of these solutions don't _____ the current economic need.
2. So, let's put that plan _____.
3. Every advertising company wants their products to _____.
4. She spent four years studying for her degree. _____, she continued to work at a bank.
5. They are interviewing three _____ for the post of sales manager.
6. The poor economic situation has _____ investment in new technology.
7. _____ what I've been telling you all along.
8. Our _____ is the same as that of other companies.

STEP 4 ROLE-PLAY

Choose either A or B and have a conversation with your partner according to the directions. Then, switch roles and repeat the conversation.

A
- Ask B which candidate is better.
- Tell B that we need to choose the one who will fit well with our company.
- Ask B why he or she is hesitating to hire him or her.
- Tell B that you will give him or her an offer first.

B
- Tell A that they are both qualified.
- Tell A that one candidate is better than the other.
- Tell A that he or she might want a higher salary than expected.
- Tell A that you have the same idea.

UNIT 02
Interview with a Training manager

HiEnglish

STEP 1 PREPARATION

Andrea is a training manager for a human resources department. Dylan is interviewing her. Listen to the conversation and answer the following questions.

1 What do you think Dylan's job is?

2 What does Andrea do as a training manager?

3 What kind of training programs does Andrea run?

STEP 2 LISTENING

Listen to the conversation again and fill in as many blanks as you can.

Dylan	So Andrea, tell _____ _____ _____ _____ about your job as a training manager.
Andrea	Well, basically, I'm responsible for the effective planning and execution of training and development programs _____ _____ _____ _____.
Dylan	I see. And what exactly does that entail?
Andrea	Quite a lot, actually. Let's see ... I consider the _____ _____ in order to drive training initiatives. I also identify the range suitable training solutions for employees. This means I need to _____ _____ _____ all aspect of the training programs to educate people on standard processes and to enhance performance according to the needs of the company.
Dylan	And what kind of programs _____ _____ _____?
Andrea	We run the full gamut really – quality control, work measurement, human resources, manufacturing methods, _____ _____ _____, you name it.
Dylan	Okay. Can you tell us more about some of your specific duties?
Andrea	Sure. For example, I oversee the development of training content _____ _____ _____ _____ course outlines.

8 BUSINESS PIONEER 2

STEP 3 LANGUAGE DEVELOPMENT

Complete the sentences with the right expressions from the box below.

① responsible for
② basically
③ execution
④ enhance
⑤ according to
⑥ quality control
⑦ you name it
⑧ oversee

1. Although the original idea was good, its _____ has been disappointing.
2. Individuals will be _____ their own personal developments which will be measured against agreed standards of business performance.
3. A steering board is being established to _____ the work.
4. He believes that organizational effectiveness is _____ by fair and ethical management.
5. Prices are variable _____ the rate of exchange.
6. _____, these are the database administrator's tasks.
7. He owns sport teams, cable companies, _____.
8. The _____ process did not completely eliminate defective products.

STEP 4 ROLE-PLAY

Choose either A or B and have a conversation with your partner according to the directions. Then, switch roles and repeat the conversation.

A
- Ask B what he or she does as a training manager.
- Ask B what he or she does in more detail.
- Ask B what kind of programs he or she runs.
- Ask B what his or her specific duties are.

B
- Tell B what you do.
- Explain to B what you do in more detail.
- Tell B about the programs you run.
- Tell B about your duties.

Review expressions

I Match the words (1-8) to the definitions (a-h).

qualified	1	a	to develop all the details of a plan for doing something
fit	2	b	how successful someone or something is
formulate	3	c	having the skills, qualities, or experience that you need
entail	4	d	the whole range of things of that kind
initiative	5	f	an important new plan or process to achieve a particular aim or to solve a particular problem
performance	6	e	a person who supervises workers
gamut	7	g	to involve someting as a necessary part or result
supervisor	8	h	to be adapted to or suitable for

II Complete the sentences with the words above.

1 The company has hired a financial adviser to assist in _____ a growth strategy.

2 What did the _____ say about extending the deadline?

3 The company had poor _____ for the first two years.

4 They do not _____ well in any organization.

5 This was important because many of the staff did not fully understand what the role _____.

6 The cost-cutting _____ are expected to result in savings of $300 million.

7 The network will provide a full _____ of computer services to your home.

8 I must recognize that I am not _____ for the post.

Section 1 Job

CHAPTER 02

Finance & Accounting

WARM UP

1 What comes to mind when you hear the words "finance" and "accounting?"

2 What do a company's financial statements tell you?

3 How does your company generate revenue? What's your company's cash cow business?

Unit 01

HiEnglish

Reporting First Half Profits

STEP 1 PREPARATION

Several employees are having a meeting to go over profits in the first half. Shelly suggests looking for new clients instead of depending on a few big ones. Listen to the conversation and answer the following questions.

1. Who is Treestar? What does Mike say about this company?

2. How does Emily suggest to get more clients?

3. What will Emily email to all of the staff in the meeting?

STEP 2 LISTENING

Listen to the conversation again and fill in as many blanks as you can.

Mike	Today, we're going to discuss our targets _____ _____ _____ _____. Treestar is still our largest client by far. We need to keep _____ _____ _____ _____ them, of course.
Shelly	But we can't just depend on them. What happens if they leave us?
Emily	Shelly is right. We need to _____ _____ getting more business from smaller clients so that we remain stable even if we lose Treestar.
Mike	How do you suggest we do that, Emily?
Emily	I guess the first thing we need to do is to _____ _____ what cases we've handled for other clients and how much money we made from each.
Mike	Does everyone know how to do that?
Emily	I can email all of you a file that _____ _____ _____ _____ how to write the report if you want.
Mike	That would be great.

STEP 3 LANGUAGE DEVELOPMENT

Complete the sentences with the right expressions from the box below.

① by far
② take good care of
③ concentrate on
④ remain stable
⑤ even if
⑥ look into
⑦ detailed information
⑧ write the report

1 For _____, please refer to the attached product guide. Feel free to ask me any questions regarding the product.
2 What's wrong with you today? You don't seem to be _____ your work.
3 Do you know who _____ about our competitors?
4 That's too bad. I hope you will get well soon. Please _____ yourself.
5 Ms. Robinson has good leadership skills. She is _____ the best executive in the company.
6 Our profit growth will _____ this year and will hopefully remain at last year's level.
7 What you did to Jill was horrible. _____ you apologize, she still may not forgive you.
8 We're _____ the possibility of merging the two departments at the moment.

STEP 4 ROLE-PLAY

Choose either A or B and have a conversation with your partner according to the directions. Then, switch roles and repeat the conversation.

A
- Ask B what the two of you will discuss.
- Tell B that the company has to keep taking good care of its large clients to meet these targets.
- Ask B what B's suggestion is to fix this.
- Ask B how you can help.
- Ask B if his or her team knows how to do that.

B
- Tell A that you're going to discuss the targets for first half profits.
- Tell A that the company relies too much on these big companies.
- Answer A.
- Answer A.
- Tell A that you will email them about it.

CHAPTER 02 Finance & Accounting 13

UNIT 02
Confirming Settlement of Accounts

HiEnglish

STEP 1 PREPARATION

Gabriella works in the accounting team. She wants to use some vacation days, so she's asking the team manager for approval. Listen to the conversation and answer the following questions.

1. How many days does Gabriella want for her vacation?

2. What has Gabriella been working on?

3. How does Gabriella suggest to finish the work on time?

STEP 2 LISTENING

Listen to the conversation again and fill in as many blanks as you can.

Gabriella	Excuse me, Ito. Since you're our department's manager, I was hoping I could _____ _____ _____ to use three of my vacation days at the start of December.
Ito	Sure, but how is the fiscal year report you've been working on? The deadline is getting closer.
Gabriella	I've already completed _____ _____ _____ it. I can send you the final draft by tomorrow morning.
Ito	That's good to hear. But there are still a few more tasks that must be finished before the end of the month, and I'm worried that the report _____ _____ _____ _____ _____ without you.
Gabriella	That won't be an issue. I'm willing to _____ _____ _____ _____ and finish it before I leave.
Ito	Great. That would be very helpful. I'll see to it that you receive the necessary assignments right away.
Gabriella	Thank you.
Ito	As long as the budget is finished by tomorrow, then there shouldn't be a problem if _____ _____ during that time.

STEP 3 LANGUAGE DEVELOPMENT

Complete the sentences with the right expressions from the box below.

① approval to
② work on
③ final draft
④ be completed
⑤ be an issue
⑥ be willing to
⑦ take on extra work
⑧ as long as

1. As you know, it's a large-scale project. We're still _____ it.
2. I don't think it's going to _____. We can definitely get them ready by Tuesday.
3. Well, I can't say offhand. I'll have to check and get my boss's _____ proceed.
4. How soon can you send us the _____? Please send it no later than the 3rd.
5. _____ our company reaches 35 percent of the market this year, the CEO will be happy.
6. That's way overpriced. I _____ not _____ pay $500 for a tiny lamp. It's insane.
7. The project is expected to _____ by the end of this month. At last, I'm beginning to see daylight.
8. We haven't found a suitable person to take over for Jessica yet. I'm sorry but you may need to _____ for a while.

STEP 4 ROLE-PLAY

Choose either A or B and have a conversation with your partner according to the directions. Then, switch roles and repeat the conversation.

A

- Tell B that you want to get approval to use your vacation days.
- Tell B that you're done with your portion of it.
- Ask B if there is any issue.
- Tell B that you're willing to take on extra work and finish it before you leave.
- Thank B.

B

- Tell A that you are okay with that, but that the deadline for the fiscal year is getting closer.
- Tell A that there are still a few more tasks to be finished by the end of this month.
- Tell A that you're worried that the report won't be completed on time without A.
- Thank A and tell him or her that you'll find some assignments for A to do.
- Tell A that everything is fine as long as the budget is finished by tomorrow.

Review expressions

I Match the words (1-8) to the definitions (a-h).

target	1	a	a task or a piece of work that is given to someone to do
concentrate	2	b	official permission or agreement for something
remain	3	c	result, level, or situation that an organization wants or plans to achieve
stable	4	d	to give all of your attention to one particular activity, subject, or problem
approval	5	e	a part or share of something larger
fiscal year	6	f	to stay in the same place or in the same condition
portion	7	g	able to continue in a regular and successful way without unexpected changes
assignment	8	h	a period of 12 months for which a company prepares its accounts

II Complete the sentences with the words above.

1 We always set a _____ at the beginning of the year.
2 Why would you do that? It's a big risk to leave a _____ job.
3 I really can't _____ on my work with all that noise from outside.
4 The new strategy hasn't received _____ from the board yet.
5 We certainly have to invest more in new technology if we are to _____ competitive in the market.
6 Our company is UK based and its _____ runs from 6th April to the following 5th April.
7 I donate a small _____ of my income to children's charities every month.
8 Our team was given an _____ to analyze the client database.

Section 1 Job

CHAPTER 03

Sales

WARM UP

1 Why do you choose one product over another? When you buy something, do you "shop around" and compare prices?

2 There are a range of different sales promotions. Name some. What kind of sales promotions are you receptive to?

3 Have you worked in sales before? What qualities make a good salesperson?

Unit 01

Domestic Sales

HiEnglish

STEP 1 PREPARATION

Samantha's team is having a weekly sales meeting. James is describing a goal for this month, and the other share their opinions on it. Listen to the conversation and answer the following questions.

1 What is the goal of this team?

2 What promotion did Samantha suggest? What about Bruce?

3 Which idea do you think is best?

STEP 2 LISTENING

Listen to the conversation again and fill in as many blanks as you can.

Samantha	Now, there is _____ _____ _____ I wish to discuss before we conclude our weekly sales meeting. This is going to be a very busy month for all of us. James, what's our goal?
James	We're aiming to _____ _____ _____ this month.
Samantha	Right. The reason we're anticipating this increase in business is the _____-_____-_____-_____-_____ promotion we are offering in our branches.
Bruce	How long does it last?
James	The promotion will last _____ _____ _____ _____ _____.
Samantha	We need all of your customers to be aware that this offer lasts _____ _____ _____ _____ _____.
Bruce	What about the flyers? It could draw attention and give information about our promotion.
Samantha	Alright, let's give it a try! Please make sure to _____ _____ _____ to anyone that comes in to our branches.

18 BUSINESS PIONEER 2

STEP 3 LANGUAGE DEVELOPMENT

Complete the sentences with the right expressions from the box below.

① for all of us
② aim to
③ record sales
④ buy-one-get-one-free
⑤ be aware
⑥ for a limited time
⑦ draw attention
⑧ give it a try

1. It's okay to make mistakes. Don't hesitate, just _____.
2. Our group achieved _____ and operating results in the UK last year. It was truly a commendable performance.
3. Have you seen this? Electro offers _____ even on already sale items!
4. In order to get rid of excess stock, we _____ bring down prices 60% on all our computers manufactured two or more years ago.
5. Sales promotions are vital for companies to increase sales and project their brand names. They _____ to a particular product or service being offered.
6. There are 15 people in our team already. Our dinner budget is just too little _____.
7. As you may _____, our company is going to downsize due to the bad economy.
8. These offers are available to members _____. Do not miss out!

STEP 4 ROLE-PLAY

Choose either A or B and have a conversation with your partner according to the directions. Then, switch roles and repeat the conversation.

A
- Tell B about the last issue to discuss. (the goal of the sales this month)
- Tell B about the promotion.
  (Promotion: buy-one-get-one-free)
- Answer B.
- Ask B about flyers.
- Answer B's question.

B
- Tell A that your goal is to reach record sales this month.
- Ask A how long it will last.
- Tell A that all your customers should be aware of this offer.
- Ask A if they will be effective.
- Agree with A.

Unit 02
International Sales

STEP 1 PREPARATION

Antonio and Monica's company just acquired a Japanese software firm. Antonio has dreams of working abroad. Listen to the conversation and answer the following questions.

1. Where did Monica get the news about the acquisition of the company?

2. What will Antonio do to work in Japan?

3. How can Antonio overcome the language barrier?

STEP 2 LISTENING

Listen to the conversation again and fill in as many blanks as you can.

Antonio Hi, Monica, were you in today's staff meeting this morning? I wanted to attend, but I was with a client.

Monica Yes, I was. The director _____ _____ _____ _____. Our company finally acquired the renowned Japanese software company, Seiko Corporation.

Antonio Is there any chance to be transferred to Japan? I _____ _____ _____ working abroad for a long time.

Monica Oh, really? Yes, you can apply. _____ _____ _____ we will expand in the country.

Antonio Well, it'd depend on the circumstances, but _____ _____ _____ _____ it.

Monica What about the language? You might need _____ _____ for the sales in Japan.

Antonio I took Japanese classes in university for about three years.

Monica That's great! Good luck!

STEP 3 LANGUAGE DEVELOPMENT

Complete the sentences with the right expressions from the box below.

① special announcement
② software company
③ transfer to
④ work abroad
⑤ for a long time
⑥ apply
⑦ sooner or later
⑧ be open to

1 I've got a new job at this _____, NESIM. It's been my dream company to work for since I was a teenager.
2 Jenny looked somewhat upset. It seemed like she _____ not _____ any other suggestions.
3 I have a very _____ to make! Our company successfully arranged a $100 million investment.
4 I _____ for this job since it is an excellent match for my skills and abilities and is similar to my previous professional experiences.
5 I heard through the grapevine that Satin would go bankrupt _____. Do you know anything about it?
6 Would there be any opportunities for me to _____? I'd like to improve my career prospects.
7 We've been looking for a partner _____. Our ideal partner is an experienced SAP professional consultant with over twenty years of experience.
8 I'm going to _____ one of the branches in Europe next month but please don't tell anybody yet.

STEP 4 ROLE-PLAY

Choose either A or B and have a conversation with your partner according to the directions. Then, switch roles and repeat the conversation.

A
- Ask B how today's staff meeting was this morning.
- Answer B.
- Ask B if you can apply for relocation to Japan.
- Tell B that you've been wanting to work overseas.
- Answer B. (You don't have any problem with the language.)

B
- Answer A and ask A why he or she was absent.
- Tell A that the director announced the successful acquisition of a Japanese company.
- Answer A that there will be a position available soon.
- Ask A about his or her language skills.
- Wish A good luck.

Review expressions

I Match the words (1-8) to the definitions (a-h).

record	1	a	at some time in the future
buy-one-get-one-free	2	b	a small piece of paper with information on it about a product or event
last	3	c	something that someone says officially, giving information about something
flyer	4	d	an offer used in shops, in which if you buy one thing, you get another of the same thing for no extra cost
announcement	5	e	at a higher level than ever achieved before
renowned	6	f	to continue to exist
sooner or later	7	g	a job, especially one that is important
position	8	h	famous for something

II Complete the sentences with the words above.

1 The meeting _____ more than two hours. It was the most unproductive meeting ever!

2 We hope to fill the marketing _____ within the next two months.

3 Our CEO made an unexpected _____ this morning.

4 My job is to hand out _____ for the newly opened sushi restaurant on street corners.

5 Unemployment rate has reached a _____ high in this year.

6 MLink has been selected as a preferred supplier by major, highly _____ companies such as Samsung and Hyundai Motors via online survey.

7 I just can't resist those _____ deals.

8 It's true that we're not in an extreme hurry at the moment but _____ we have to choose among the options.

Section 1 Job

CHAPTER 04

Advertising & Marketing

WARM UP

1 What kind of product/service does your company provide? What's your company's target market? Describe in detail.

2 What are some effective ads you've seen lately (on TV, newspaper, etc.)? What makes an ad memorable?

3 Which advertisements do you like the most and the least? Why? Do you buy products because of advertising?

Unit 01

HiEnglish

Advertising Concept

STEP 1 PREPARATION

Carol and Manuel are talking about an upcoming advertising campaign. There is one thing to decide. Listen to the conversation and answer the following questions.

1 What is the advertising campaign about?

2 What did the marketing team ask?

3 Why can't Manuel send it to the print shop until next week?

STEP 2 LISTENING

Listen to the conversation again and fill in as many blanks as you can.

Carol	Is the advertising campaign for our new product _____ _____ according to schedule?
Manuel	Yes, it is proceeding alright.
Carol	It is an important product of our company's this year, so we have to _____ _____ _____ _____ a good job. Have you discussed the ad with the marketing team yet?
Manuel	Yes, and they're _____ _____ everything except for the background color. They've asked us to change it from dark blue to dark green.
Carol	Can we have it done on time?
Manuel	Once we've done that, it'll be ready to be sent to the print shop. We have _____ _____ _____.
Carol	Okay, but just keep in mind that we won't be able to send it out to them until next week. I heard that the print shop had to send out some printing equipment for repair, so they're _____ _____ _____ _____.
Manuel	Oh, I'll check it out.

24 BUSINESS PIONEER 2

STEP 3 LANGUAGE DEVELOPMENT

Complete the sentences with the right expressions from the box below.

① come along
② according to
③ be pleased with
④ except for
⑤ print shop
⑥ plenty of
⑦ keep in mind
⑧ send out

1. We've been engaged in this business for over twenty years. We have _____ experience in this area.
2. All our team members are going to attend Jenny's farewell party _____ John. He said he's going on a business trip.
3. I think I'll go to lunch now. Would you like to _____ with me?
4. _____ that this proposal is only a draft. There is room for negotiation on this.
5. Check this out. _____ these documents, you still owe us $3,000.
6. Can you go pick up our flyers from the _____? It's on the second floor of the red building across the street.
7. Now, let's put it in writing and sign it. Thank you for choosing our company. I'm sure you'll _____ our product.
8. We're not in charge of that. Monthly statements are _____ by the financial team.

STEP 4 ROLE-PLAY

Choose either A or B and have a conversation with your partner according to the directions. Then, switch roles and repeat the conversation.

A
- Ask B if the ad campaign is coming along according to schedule.
- Ask B if they discussed the ad with the marketing team.
- Ask B if the marketing team asked to change it.
- Ask B if there is enough time for that.
- Tell B to send it to the print shop once it's done.

B
- Tell A that it's proceeding alright.
- Tell A that they were pleased with everything except for the background color.
- Tell A that they wanted to change it to dark green.
- Tell A that there is.
- Tell A that you will.

Unit 02

Marketing Target & Method

HiEnglish

STEP 1 PREPARATION

Gwen and Alex are talking about the second quarter's sales figure, but it is not as good as they expected. Alex suggests a solution. Listen to the conversation and answer the following questions.

1. What caused the poor sales performance?

2. How did Alex reach his conclusion?

3. What kind of advertising method are they using?

STEP 2 LISTENING

Listen to the conversation again and fill in as many blanks as you can.

Gwen　So how was the second quarter's sales figure?

Alex　According to the sales report, our new product has not sold as well as _____ _____ _____.

Gwen　Why was there such poor performance?

Alex　After analyzing the data, we've _____ _____ _____ _____ _____ that we are not effectively reaching our target customer base for this product.

Gwen　What age group _____ _____ _____ _____?

Alex　Well, as we're talking about various accessories for electronic devices such as Bluetooth keyboards and speakers, we targeted consumers between 20 and 30 years old. But the sales are much _____ _____ _____ _____.

Gwen　What about the marketing method? Is it still effective?

Alex　The marketing team still believes TV ads are the only way to show _____ _____ _____ _____ the products are, but I'm not convinced.

26 BUSINESS PIONEER 2

STEP 3 LANGUAGE DEVELOPMENT

Complete the sentences with the right expressions from the box below.

① sales figures
② sales report
③ come to a conclusion
④ target customer base
⑤ aim at
⑥ such as
⑦ marketing method
⑧ TV ads

1. Your _____ is, without a doubt, one of the most important elements of your restaurant. Your customers determine your success.
2. My company has made rubber products, _____ waterproof rain coats and boots since the early 1800s.
3. The meeting lasted well into the night but we still couldn't _____.
4. We have decided not to disclose initial _____ to the public at this time.
5. The main reason _____ is so effective is the size of the audience it reaches. Nearly every Korean household has a television set.
6. I put the _____ right on my desk, but it's gone! I need it for a meeting.
7. Our new advertising campaign is specifically _____ young people between the ages of 14 and 19.
8. Every business is differnt, so not every _____ is going to be effective.

STEP 4 ROLE-PLAY

Choose either A or B and have a conversation with your partner according to the directions. Then, switch roles and repeat the conversation.

A
- Ask B how the second quarter's sales were. (Product: accessories for electronic devices)
- Ask B why sales underperformed.
- Ask B what aged consumers he or she aimed at.
- Tell B that's why the sales were much lower than your projections.
- Ask B about the marketing method.

B
- Tell A that it was not as good as you had anticipated.
- Answer A.
- Answer A.
- Agree to A's opinion.
- Tell A that the marketing team only has TV ads.

CHAPTER 04 Advertising & Marketing

REVIEW EXPRESSIONS

I Match the words (1-8) to the definitions (a-h).

advertising campaign	1	a	a device that accomplishes its purpose electronically
according to	2	b	a group of ads centralized around one message
except	3	c	to imagine or expect that something will happen
repair	4	d	as stated, reported, or recorded by someone or something
anticipate	5	e	a calculation or guess about the future based on information that you have
target customer	6	f	not including, but not
electronic device	7	g	the type of person that a company wants to sell its products or services to
projection	8	h	the act of fixing something that is broken or damaged

II Complete the sentences with the words above.

1 We all know that it's best to _____ problems before they arise but it's not easy as it sounds.

2 There's nothing like a good _____ to boost sales.

3 _____ include televisions, DVD players, laptops, desktop computers, mobile phones, iPods, iPads, cameras and more.

4 Sales _____ made last year were too optimistic.

5 My car broke down last week. It is still at the garage for _____.

6 _____ our CEO, our firm is expected to have sales of more than $2 billion this year.

7 Pepsi's traditional _____ are teenagers and young adults.

8 Our offices are open Monday through Friday _____ on national holidays.

Section 1 Job

CHAPTER 05

Production & Manufacturing

WARM UP

1 Have you ever visited a factory and seen a production line? Share your experience with the class.

2 Have you ever received damaged goods or an item you didn't order? How did you feel? How did you handle the situation?

3 Do you know how to deal with an angry client or a frustrated customer who is upset about a delivery?

UNIT 01

HiEnglish

Talking About Output

STEP 1 PREPARATION

Tristan's just got a call from the warehouse about a product. So, he is checking this out with Cecilia. Listen to the conversation and answer the following questions.

1. What is the problem?

2. What was the warehouse manager concerned about?

3. What percentage of the product was produced so far?

STEP 2 LISTENING

Listen to the conversation again and fill in as many blanks as you can.

Tristan	The warehouse just called. They said they're still waiting to receive _____ _____ _____ _____ a product. Is there something wrong with the production line at our plant?
Cecilia	Well, there seems to be a problem with the labeling machine because the product labels aren't _____ _____ the surface of the product. The technician is _____ _____ _____ to take a look at them.
Tristan	Did you report this to the warehouse manager?
Cecilia	Yes, I already informed him. He was concerned about _____ _____ _____. How much has been produced so far?
Tristan	Actually, less than 70 percent.
Cecilia	It sounds like we should _____ _____ as soon as possible.
Tristan	Right. Please give me a call with an update once you speak with the technician.
Cecilia	Sure, I will.

30 BUSINESS PIONEER 2

STEP 3 LANGUAGE DEVELOPMENT

Complete the sentences with the right expressions from the box below.

① warehouse
② batch of
③ stick to
④ on one's way
⑤ be concerned about
⑥ make the deadline
⑦ sound like
⑧ resume production

1. Please tell Johnny I'm _____ to the office. It won't take long.
2. I'm already having a hard time. Should I _____ that too?
3. Oh, no! Not again. We must _____ no matter what this time. It's a matter of credibility.
4. It _____ a great opportunity for our company. Let's review the details.
5. Due to a strike at our factory, we will not be able to supply the items you need immediately. Unfortunately, we're not sure when we will _____ again.
6. I don't know why this post-it note doesn't _____ anything. I should've bought the Super Sticky one.
7. Five _____ raw material for our product will be delivered later today.
8. Our _____ was built in 1980. It's time to undergo extensive renovations.

STEP 4 ROLE-PLAY

Choose either A or B and have a conversation with your partner according to the directions. Then, switch roles and repeat the conversation.

A

- Tell B that you've got a call from the warehouse which is still waiting to receive a product.
- Ask B what the problem is exactly.
- Ask B how they handled it.
- Ask B what total production is so far.
- Tell B that we should resume production as soon as possible.

B

- Tell A that there seems to be a problem in the plant.
- Tell A that the labeling machine doesn't work properly.
- Tell A that you called the technician and he is on the way.
- Answer A.
- Agree with A and promise to update him or her once you speak with the technician.

Unit 02

HiEnglish

Apologizing for Delay

STEP 1 PREPARATION

Jane just called Fast Export Company to file a complaint. Russel answers the phone. Listen to the conversation and answer the following questions.

1 What is Jane's complaint?

2 Why does Jane need the product quickly?

3 How does Jane want to receive the product?

STEP 2 LISTENING

Listen to the conversation again and fill in as many blanks as you can.

Russel	Good morning. Fast Export Company. How can I help you?
Jane	I'm afraid I _____ _____ _____ _____ about your last delivery of products.
Russel	Oh, what's the problem? I hope the delivery arrived on time.
Jane	Yes, it was on time, but unfortunately _____ _____ _____ _____.
Russel	Oh, I'm sorry to hear that. And the products?
Jane	I'm afraid a few items are defective. I know you would replace them if we _____ _____ _____, but it's getting close to the holidays, and we need the products urgently.
Russel	I understand. I'll pass on your complaints to the packaging department.
Jane	Sorry, but you really have to fix this for me today. It's _____ _____. If it wasn't so urgent, I wouldn't call you, but we need the products now. I would be grateful if you sent the missing items immediately _____ _____ _____.

STEP 3 LANGUAGE DEVELOPMENT

Complete the sentences with the right expressions from the box below.

① have a serious complaint
② arrive on time
③ be damaged
④ send ... back
⑤ get close
⑥ pass on
⑦ would be grateful if
⑧ by express delivery

1. We can't find any fault on our part. The products were fine when they left here. Please _____ them _____ to us so we can inspect them.
2. I will have it sent to you immediately. It will _____.
3. He hasn't called you back yet? I _____ your message this morning. He must be very busy at the moment.
4. Can I speak to your supervisor, please? I _____ to make about the hygiene of your hotel.
5. I'm calling with some bad news. I'm afraid some of the goods _____ during shipment.
6. I _____ you could send your schedule via email.
7. It's _____ to my birthday. Only three more days to go! I will take a day off on that day.
8. How quickly can you deliver the product we ordered? We want you to ship it _____ as soon as possible.

STEP 4 ROLE-PLAY

Choose either A or B and have a conversation with your partner according to the directions. Then, switch roles and repeat the conversation.

A
- Tell B that you have a complaint about the delivery of some products.
- Tell B that the packaging was damaged.
- Tell B that some items are defective, so you want to send them back.
- Tell B that it is extremely urgent because the holidays are coming.
- Tell B that you want A to send the items immediately by express delivery.

B
- Ask A what the problem is.
- Apologize to A and ask about the products.
- Ask A by when they need the products.
- Tell A that you will pass on A's complaints to the packaging department.

Review expressions

I Match the words (1-8) to the definitions (a-h).

warehouse	1	a	without any delay	
plant	2	b	a statement that you are unhappy or not satisfied with something	
inform	3	c	the act of taking goods, letters, parcels, etc. to people's houses or places of work	
resume	4	d	a large building for storing things before they are sold, used, or sent out to stores	
complaint	5	e	a factory or other place where goods are manufactured	
delivery	6	f	to tell someone about particular facts	
replace	7	g	to start something again after a pause or period of time	
immediately	8	h	to provide a new one	

II Complete the sentences with the words above.

1 The new company policy will become effective _____.
2 Our company has developed a system to handle customer _____ and introduced it early this month.
3 Coop guarantees product _____ within 24 hours of purchase for orders of $10 or more, even on the holidays.
4 I recently _____ the old rug in the living room with a new one.
5 There was a huge fire at the manufacturing _____ last year but no one was killed.
6 Why wasn't I _____ about this earlier? I'm so disappointed.
7 The meeting isn't over yet. It will be _____ after taking a short break.
8 They are planning to pull down the _____ to build a new supermarket.

Section 1 Job

CHAPTER 06

Quality Control

WARM UP

1 Why is quality important for a business?

2 What would happen to a company's sales if it did not practice quality control?

3 Have you ever bought a defective product? What kind of defect was it? How did you handle the situation?

UNIT 01

HiEnglish

Talking About Defect Rate

STEP 1 PREPARATION

Mr. Kwan's plant has a high defect rate. Vicky and Jasmine are looking for a solution. Listen to the conversation and answer the following questions.

1. What percentage of Mr. Kwan's line is defective?

2. What did Mr. Kwan ask Vicky to do?

3. What do they have to do in order to find the cause of the defects?

STEP 2 LISTENING

Listen to the conversation again and fill in as many blanks as you can.

Vicky	During our last discussion, Mr. Kwan wanted us to visit him and _____ _____ _____. Is the defect rate still at 10%?
Jasmine	Yes. He suggested that _____ _____ _____ _____ to improve the manufacturing process.
Vicky	Have you looked at it, Michael? What's the problem?
Michael	Since Mr. Kwan's plant has several product lines, our specialist recommends that _____ _____ _____ _____. We can locate the problem within a few days, but the factory will have to shut down during that time.
Vicky	Do you think we can make the deadline if we _____ _____ _____ for a week?
Michael	Yes. Some employees can work over the weekend.
Jasmine	I'll let the managers know and find out how many employees can work overtime. If we don't have enough volunteers, we need to _____ _____ _____ _____.

36 BUSINESS PIONEER 2

STEP 3 LANGUAGE DEVELOPMENT

Complete the sentences with the right expressions from the box below.

① manufacturing process
② product line
③ inspect every one
④ shut down
⑤ make the deadline
⑥ put off
⑦ work overtime
⑧ hire some temporary employees

1. Robots and machines cannot replace the whole _____ because they lack the sensitivity of human hands.
2. At this rate, everything will come to nothing. It's impossible to _____. Can we postpone it somehow?
3. I never _____ today's work until the next day. I'm a very organized and focused person.
4. Who likes to _____? But if I have to do it, I will.
5. Our company _____ through an agency during the busy season.
6. For everyone's safety, our warehouse in Northern Seoul will _____ for a yearlong renovation.
7. Expanding our _____ can be an effective way to grow our brand, reach new customers, and increase loyalty.
8. I understand that I am to _____ of our products for malfunctions.

STEP 4 ROLE-PLAY

Choose either A or B and have a conversation with your partner according to the directions. Then, switch roles and repeat the conversation.

A
- Tell B that there are still some defective items.
- Ask B what the problem is.
- Ask B if the specialist should go check it.
- Ask B if the factory needs to close down.
- Tell B that the deadline is just around the corner.

B
- Describe to A the actions you took to fix this.
- Answer A.
- Tell A your specialist already did.
- Tell A that you need a few days to figure out the problem.
- Tell A that you can work on weekends until the deadline is met.

UNIT 02

HiEnglish

Talking About the Quality

STEP 1 PREPARATION

Carol just discovered the low quality of a product after visiting the factory in which it is made. She is asking Kevin about a solution. Listen to the conversation and answer the following questions.

1 What is the problem in the assembly line?

2 What can you tell about the machine in Carol's factory?

3 What does Kevin need to do before purchasing a new machine?

STEP 2 LISTENING

Listen to the conversation again and fill in as many blanks as you can.

Carol	I just came back from the assembly line, and _____ _____ _____ _____ something wrong with the case for our product. It is too thick.
Kevin	That's not good. I also noticed yesterday that the exterior finishing of our final product wasn't as thin and even _____ _____ _____ _____.
Carol	The problem needs to be figured out quickly.
Kevin	I wonder _____ _____ _____ _____. Do you think it might be molding?
Carol	Hmm … That machine is very old, and it was repaired _____ _____ _____ _____. Maybe it's finally time to buy a new one.
Kevin	As you know, we have to _____ _____ _____ _____ _____ the purchase, so I'll talk to him about it.
Carol	When can I know? I need to inform the other managers of this issue.
Kevin	I'll call you in the afternoon and confirm if _____ _____ _____ _____ _____.

STEP 3 LANGUAGE DEVELOPMENT

Complete the sentences with the right expressions from the box below.

① come back from
② assembly line
③ figure out
④ cause the problem
⑤ quite a few times
⑥ get one's approval
⑦ it's time to
⑧ inform ... of

1. I may have _____. Please accept my apology.
2. Whatever your idea is, you need to _____ your boss's _____ first.
3. I think _____ not the right _____ talk about the issue. Can we bring it up at the next team meeting?
4. We are trying to keep the _____ running while the inspection is being done.
5. Mr. Verdi hasn't _____ the meeting yet. Would you like to leave a message for him?
6. My brand new computer keeps crashing! I have to _____ what the problem is.
7. You mean the new seafood buffet across the street? I've already been there _____.
8. Your email is used as a login to access your account, and also to _____ you _____ the progress of your orders.

STEP 4 ROLE-PLAY

Choose either A or B and have a conversation with your partner according to the directions. Then, switch roles and repeat the conversation.

A
- Tell B that you just came back from the assembly line and found something wrong with the casing.
- Tell B that the case is too thick.
- Tell B that you need to figure out the cause.
- Tell B that the machine is very old and it was fixed several times.
- Tell B that he or she has to get approval from the director first.

B
- Ask A what the problem is.
- Tell A that you noticed the same problem yesterday.
- Tell A that the molding could cause the problem.
- Suggest that A buy a new one.
- Tell A that you will talk to the director.

Review expressions

I Match the words (1-8) to the definitions (a-h).

defective	1		a	after the usual time needed or expected in a job
inspect	2		b	about or relating to
operation	3		c	official permission or agreement for something
overtime	4		d	to look at something carefully in order to check its quality or condition
assembly line	5		e	containing a fault, or not working correctly
approval	6		f	a manufacturing process in which interchangeable parts are added to a product in a sequential manner to create an end product
regarding	7		g	to tell someone about something, especially officially
inform	8		h	the activities involved in a company producing goods or delivering services

II Complete the sentences with the words above.

1 The company will shut down its _____, effective immediately.
2 Make sure you _____ the goods before signing for them.
3 We don't accept returns on any technology products unless they're _____ or damaged.
4 The worst job I ever had in my life was when I worked on an _____ when I was about 19.
5 Ma'am, may I ask what this is _____?
6 Factory workers were asked to work _____ to get the job done on time.
7 The project has finally received _____ from the government.
8 Our company isn't recruiting new employees at the moment. I'll _____ you of any openings.

Section 1 Job

CHAPTER 07

Materials

WARM UP

1. Does your job involve purchasing materials for your company's products? Do you know the process of purchasing materials?

2. What would you do if you cannot meet a deadline due to a delayed shipment of materials for your products? How would you handle the situation?

3. Have you ever placed an order with an overseas supplier? Did you have any trouble doing so?

Unit 01

HiEnglish

Purchasing Materials

STEP 1 PREPARATION

Denis is looking for a supplier who can provide the materials he needs. Listen to the conversation and answer the following questions.

1. Why did Denis choose this supplier?

2. What product is Denis's company developing?

3. What will Denis do before purchasing the material?

STEP 2 LISTENING

Listen to the conversation again and fill in as many blanks as you can.

Denis	Hi, I'm calling to see if I could _____ _____ _____ _____ the special material made by your company. I'm working for a local production plant, HNC, and my work involves purchasing materials for our new product.
Ellen	Well, all of our items are made with _____ _____. And we also make sure that no pollutants are produced in the manufacturing process.
Denis	My manager would definitely _____ _____ _____ that. We are developing an eco-friendly product.
Ellen	Yes, many firms are these days, so we have become popular all _____ _____ _____ _____.
Denis	But it's hard to imagine that items made of recycled materials could come in many varieties. Do you have _____ _____ _____ _____ styles?
Ellen	As a matter of fact, we do. We offer a variety of sizes and colors, just like regular materials.
Denis	Can I see some for myself?
Ellen	Sure, I'll mail some brochures of _____ _____ _____ to you. I'm sure you'll like them.

STEP 3 LANGUAGE DEVELOPMENT

Complete the sentences with the right expressions from the box below.

① be calling to
② get information
③ work for
④ recycled materials
⑤ be impressed by
⑥ eco-friendly
⑦ all over the country
⑧ as a matter of fact

1. C-mart has the best selection of _____ detergent in stock. I'll go there after work today.
2. Our main office is in Seoul, but we have branches _____.
3. This is my second order from your company. I've _____ both your product and customer service. Thanks again.
4. I feel the same way. _____, I had a similar experience.
5. I've always wanted to _____ a big international company. I don't want to miss the chance.
6. Alta went green by using _____ to make their products, which are functional, stylish, and Earth-friendly.
7. I'm interested in your latest product and want to know more details. How can I _____ about it?
8. Good morning, Mr. Shin. I _____ confirm our lunch tomorrow.

STEP 4 ROLE-PLAY

Choose either A or B and have a conversation with your partner according to the directions. Then, switch roles and repeat the conversation.

A
- Introduce yourself and explain to B that you are calling to get some information. (About a special material)
- Ask B about the environment.
- Tell B that you're very impressed to hear that.
- Ask B about the selection.
- Ask B if you see some of their products.

B
- Tell A about the material. (It is made with recycled materials.)
- Tell A that no pollutants are produced in the manufacturing process.
- Tell A that many share his or her opinion, and as a result your product is very popular.
- Answer A.
- Answer A.

CHAPTER 07 Materials

UNIT 02

HiEnglish

Selling Materials

STEP 1 PREPARATION

Tiffany ran out of some parts while at work in a factory. She asks Sam if the parts are available. Listen to the conversation and answer the following questions.

1 Why couldn't Tiffany get more parts?

2 When will the parts arrive?

3 Why did Tiffany ask Sam to assure the parts would come by this week?

STEP 2 LISTENING

Listen to the conversation again and fill in as many blanks as you can.

Tiffany	Hi, Sam. We're out of parts C6 and F78 for model 6527. Could you _____ _____ _____ them here?
Sam	Actually, we ran out yesterday. I _____ _____ _____.
Tiffany	When will they arrive? I need to let the managers of each product line know about this.
Sam	The supplier called me this morning and said the shipment is _____ _____.
Tiffany	The deadline is coming up fast.
Sam	I know, and the supplier did assure me that it would be here by next week _____ _____ _____.
Tiffany	Well, I hope it will be here by this week because I guaranteed the partners' delivery by next week.
Sam	I'm not sure the supplier can do that, but I'll talk to them.
Tiffany	Thank you. Please let me know as soon as the shipment arrives so I can _____ _____ _____ _____.

STEP 3 LANGUAGE DEVELOPMENT

Complete the sentences with the right expressions from the box below.

① be out of
② run out
③ place an order
④ product line
⑤ behind schedule
⑥ at the latest
⑦ let me know
⑧ as soon as

1. Our company's _____ comprises 50 different items and this catalog covers them all.
2. The time between _____ and receiving that order is now down to one day.
3. Please pay this bill within five days _____. Otherwise a late fee will be charged.
4. We have to hurry and finish soon or we will fall _____. It is totally out of the question to postpone the deadline again.
5. I guess it will be done by tomorrow. I'll call you _____ it's ready to be picked up.
6. I haven't received my order confirmation or tracking information by email yet. Can you please _____ the status of my order?
7. Have we _____ of coffee again? Who should I ask to order more?
8. My computer is giving me an error that my printer _____ paper when it is not.

STEP 4 ROLE-PLAY

Choose either A or B and have a conversation with your partner according to the directions. Then, switch roles and repeat the conversation.

A
- Tell B that some parts ran out and ask if he or she can bring some to you.
- Ask B when they will arrive.
- Ask B why so late.
- Tell B that the deadline is coming up.
- Thank B for doing that and ask for updates.

B
- Tell A that those parts are out of stock and you placed an order yesterday.
- Tell A next week at the latest.
- Explain to A that you were told by the supplier the shipment is delayed.
- Tell A that you'll make another request to the supplier.

Review expressions

I Match the words (1-8) to the definitions (a-h).

material	1	a	a product that sells in some specifid way
recycled	2	b	a company that provides a product, or the materials to make a product
brochure	3	c	a physical substance that things can be made from
seller	4	d	to promise that something will happen or is true
shipment	5	e	a type of small magazine that contains pictures and information on a product or a company
supplier	6	f	goods being sent somewhere
guarantee	7	g	having been used before and then put through a process so that it can form a new product
request	8	h	a question in which you ask for something

II Complete the sentences with the words above.

1 A steady _____ can sometimes sell for many months and years and creates more income than the bestseller of the moment.

2 Our organic olives are packaged in _____ glass containers.

3 This video tutorial guides you through the process of making a _____ from scratch.

4 We _____ that our products are 100% safe.

5 This sculpture was made of various _____, including steel, copper wire, and rubber.

6 The firm has made a formal _____ for access to our financial records.

7 We've decided to sue our _____ for failing to fulfill their contract.

8 You are required to pay for the goods at least a week before _____.

CHAPTER 08

Research & Development

Section 1 Job

WARM UP

1 Why do you think companies carry out market research?

2 Have you ever filled out a questionnaire? What was it about? What's your opinion of this kind of market research?

3 Have you ever worked for a company that has implemented any innovative ideas? Why is it important for businesses to be innovative?

Unit 01

Market Research

STEP 1 PREPARATION

Emmett's company will attend a national IT conference in two weeks to present their new software. He is asking Kelly to review this software. Listen to the conversation and answer the following questions.

1. What did Emmett develop?

2. What does Kelly like about the software?

3. What does Kelly suggest for Emmett's presentation?

STEP 2 LISTENING

Listen to the conversation again and fill in as many blanks as you can.

Emmett	The National IT Conference _____ _____ in two weeks. Have you had time to review the software presentation I prepared? I've tried asking the other engineers in our department, but _____ _____ _____ were available.
Kelly	You mean the new training software you developed?
Emmett	Yes, the one for nurturing technical support engineers.
Kelly	Yes, I've seen it, and it seems very innovative. I especially liked the interactive activities, and I think it's great that the audience will be able to _____ _____ _____ _____.
Emmett	Exactly. I'm sure they will all be impressed when they _____ _____ _____ _____.
Kelly	There's just one thing, Emmett. _____ _____ _____ _____ the conference organizers that you'll need at least fifteen laptops for the participants. Otherwise, you will be the only one using the software.
Emmett	Thank you for the reminder. I'll let them know in advance.

STEP 3 LANGUAGE DEVELOPMENT

Complete the sentences with the right expressions from the box below.

① take place
② none of
③ technical support
④ try out
⑤ impressed
⑥ how it works
⑦ at least
⑧ otherwise

1. This is the new software that we recently developed. I'll show you exactly _____.
2. I must say, I'm _____ with the quality of the pictures that she's taken. I thought she's only an amateur.
3. I really do appreciate your concern but it's _____ your business. Please don't take it personally.
4. The copy machine is not working again. Maybe it's a paper jam. I'll contact the _____ team right away.
5. If you keep doing things the same way you always have, you will easily fall into a rut. You should be open to _____ new things.
6. The next presidential election in South Korea will _____ in 2017.
7. Okay, hold on for a second please. I'd better write it down, _____ I'll forget everything.
8. Are you really sure you can wait? It will take _____ an hour.

STEP 4 ROLE-PLAY

Choose either A or B and have a conversation with your partner according to the directions. Then, switch roles and repeat the conversation.

A
- Ask B if he or she has have time to review your presentation.
- Tell B it is and explain what your software does.
- Ask B what his or her favorite thing about it is.
- Ask B if there is anything he or her recommend for your presentation.

B
- Ask A if it is about the new training software he or she has developed.
- Tell A that you've seen it and it seems fine.
- Tell A that you like the interactive activities the most.
- Tell A your recommendation.

CHAPTER 08 Research & Development 49

UNIT 02 Checking Development Progress

HiEnglish

STEP 1 PREPARATION

Fiona is giving a status update on product development in a meeting. Listen to the conversation and answer the following questions.

1 At what stage is Fiona's development?

2 Who will be invited to the next meeting?

3 What will be discussed in the next meeting?

STEP 2 LISTENING

Listen to the conversation again and fill in as many blanks as you can.

Arius	So, Fiona, could you report _____ _____ _____ _____ your new product?
Fiona	Sure. For those who don't know me, I'm Fiona Baxter, and I work in the R&D department. We've been developing a new electric device that the company is _____ _____ _____ next quarter. At the moment, we are _____ _____ _____.
Arius	In that case, can we invite the manager of the sales team to the next meeting in order to _____ _____ _____ _____ _____ _____? This will better prepare them for future sales presentations.
Fiona	Yes, I believe so.
Arius	Great. During that meeting, why don't we also discuss the _____ _____ _____?
Fiona	I think that is a good idea. My only concern is that since the new product is _____ _____ _____ _____ than the previous models, it'll be sold at a higher price.
Arius	Alright. The agenda for the next meeting will be price determination. Please check the _____ _____ and market research data before attending.

STEP 3 LANGUAGE DEVELOPMENT

Complete the sentences with the right expressions from the box below.

① the status of
② work in
③ plan to launch
④ test product performance
⑤ in order to
⑥ market price
⑦ be more costly
⑧ product specifications

1. As our _____ indicate, the coffee maker is not designed to be used outdoors.
2. _____ get a refund, items must be returned within 30 days of purchase, together with proof of purchase.
3. The _____ of oil has gone up around 25% to $18.54 per barrel.
4. We need to _____ in order to compare our product to our competitors'.
5. Our company is _____ a catering business within a month.
6. I used to _____ the sales administration department. Now I'm in the planning department.
7. I haven't received my order yet. It's been more than one week. How do I check _____ my order?
8. Organic food tends to _____ than conventionally farmed food. Do you know why?

STEP 4 ROLE-PLAY

Choose either A or B and have a conversation with your partner according to the directions. Then, switch roles and repeat the conversation.

A
- Ask B to deliver his or her report on the development status of a new product.
- Ask B when the new product will be launched.
- Ask B if it's okay to invite the sales team to the next meeting.
- Tell B that you want to discuss the market price.
- Ask B if it should be sold at a higher price.

B
- Tell A that you've been developing a new electric device and it is in the testing stage.
- Respond to A that it will be next quarter.
- Tell A if that is okay or not.
- Explain to A that the new product is more costly to produce than the previous models.
- Suggest to A that price determination is discussed during the next meeting.

CHAPTER 08 Research & Development

REVIEW EXPRESSIONS

I Match the words (1-8) to the definitions (a-h).

engineer	1	a	the act of officially deciding something
nurture	2	b	someone who takes part in an event or activity
audience	3	c	state or condition at a particular time
participant	4	d	a person whose job is to repair or control machines, engines, or electrical equipment
status	5	e	to help a plan or a person to develop and be successful
optimum	6	f	the group of people gathered in one place to watch or listen to a play, film, someone speaking, etc.
previous	7	g	the best or most effective possible in a particular situation
determination	8	h	happening or existing before something or someone else

II Complete the sentences with the words above.

1 My father started his working life as an _____ but later became a math teacher.

2 My boss is such a confident and practiced speaker who always impresses his _____.

3 Our company needs a proper training program in order to _____ technical support engineers.

4 So, how many people are willing to attend the seminar? Are you done with the _____ list?

5 What's the _____ of my order? I haven't even got a confirmation email with a tracking number yet.

6 It never pays to talk smack about a _____ boss or employer in a job interview.

7 This document is very important as it will be used for _____ of ownership.

8 I strongly believe that is an _____ solution of all.

Section 1 | Job

CHAPTER 09

Technical Issues

WARM UP

1. How do you feel about automated call systems where you speak to a machine rather than a person?

2. What steps do you take to solve a technical problem?

3. What do you think it would be like working in a department that deals with technical issues? Could you do a job like this?

Unit 01

HiEnglish

Technical Contact

STEP 1 PREPARATION

Jeremy's computer just broke, so he called the tech department to ask for help. Listen to the conversation and answer the following questions.

1. What is the problem Jeremy has with his computer?

2. What does Tanya need to figure out Jeremy's problem?

3. Why does Jeremy ask if the technician could come before noon?

STEP 2 LISTENING

Listen to the conversation again and fill in as many blanks as you can.

Tanya Good morning, this is Tanya in the tech department. How can I help you?

Jeremy Hello, this is Jeremy Alvarez calling from the customer service department. _____ _____ _____ the Internet on my computer, and I've got to send out some important emails this morning.

Tanya Okay, I need to get your computer's serial number. It should be on a small silver sticker _____ _____ _____ _____ the unit.

Jeremy _____ _____ _____ _____. I'll take a look at it.

Tanya Take your time. Once I have that ID number, I'll _____ _____ _____ _____ _____ and send a technician this afternoon.

Jeremy I found it. It's 45129586. But would it be possible for the technician to come before noon? I have a team meeting around that time.

Tanya I see. I'll check if _____ _____ _____ before noon.

STEP 3 LANGUAGE DEVELOPMENT

Complete the sentences with the right expressions from the box below.

① can't access
② send out
③ serial number
④ on the side of
⑤ hold on a second
⑥ send a technician
⑦ before noon
⑧ be available

1. I'll be in the office all morning. You can come by anytime _____.
2. Nobody _____ to help you at the moment, but someone will definitely be here this afternoon.
3. A supervisor at Mtel just informed me that they can't _____ over to repair our Internet service today.
4. Where do I look for the _____ on my mobile phone? I need it for online activation.
5. Have you _____ the invitation yet? We're short on time.
6. All of a sudden, I _____ Yahoo, where I get my emails. I've done pretty much everything I can possibly think of and I still can't figure it out.
7. I left a notice _____ the box. Didn't you see it? It must have fallen off somehow!
8. _____, please. I need to find a pen and paper.

STEP 4 ROLE-PLAY

Choose either A or B and have a conversation with your partner according to the directions. Then, switch roles and repeat the conversation.

A

- Introduce yourself to B. (He or she is on the phone and you work in IT.)
- Ask B what the problem is.
- Tell B that you need the serial number of B's computer.
- Tell B that it would be on a silver sticker on the side of the main body.
- Tell B that the technicians are available only in the afternoon.

B

- Introduce yourself and tell A that you called due to a problem with your computer.
- Explain the problem to A.
- Ask A where the number is.
- Tell A the number and that you want a technician to visit before noon.
- Tell A that you have a meeting at 1 o'clock and ask A again if a technician can come before noon.

Unit 02

HiEnglish

Technical Support

STEP 1 PREPARATION

Ryan recently installed a new software program for merchandise inventory, but he has some issues with it. Listen to the conversation and answer the following questions.

1. Why does Ryan think the program is not very useful?

2. What was the source of the problem, according to Janice?

3. What is the solution Janice suggests to Ryan?

STEP 2 LISTENING

Listen to the conversation again and fill in as many blanks as you can.

Janice	Ryan, how is the new software that we _____ _____ to track our merchandise inventory?
Ryan	Well, to be honest, it's not very useful. Since the software updates every 36 hours, it doesn't provide the most recent information.
Janice	Oh, I see the problem. When a customer checks _____ _____ _____ an item, the inventory may show that the item is _____ _____, when in fact it's sold out.
Ryan	Hmm ... There must be a way to adjust the update frequency. I'm going to check the settings to _____ _____ _____ _____ for the inventory to be updated every 24 hours.
Janice	Make sure each item is listed only once when updating information in the system. I'd like to avoid duplicate records in the database.
Ryan	Oh, I didn't know that. Thanks for letting me know.
Janice	If you're still _____ _____, please call our team for assistance.

56 BUSINESS PIONEER 2

STEP 3 LANGUAGE DEVELOPMENT

Complete the sentences with the right expressions from the box below.

① to be honest
② since
③ the availability of
④ in fact
⑤ be sold out
⑥ update frequency
⑦ if it's possible
⑧ experience difficulties

1. How do I change the _____ for our database to once a day? Now it updates every hour and I think it's really not necessary.
2. We have to ask you for an 8% reduction. _____, it has to be 8% or there's no sale.
3. _____ model No. 203 caused problems again, we decided not to keep it in sock anymore.
4. _____, I don't really agree with the direction the business is going in these days.
5. The store down the street _____ sometimes _____ of certain groceries.
6. I can't give you any firm promises. _____ overnight delivery varies by region.
7. Who should I contact if I _____ accessing our intranet?
8. I would like to know _____ to get free room upgrades.

STEP 4 ROLE-PLAY

Choose either A or B and have a conversation with your partner according to the directions. Then, switch roles and repeat the conversation.

- Ask B how the new software you've recently installed is.
- Ask B why he or she thinks so.
- Agree with B and add that the software does not accurately represent current stock.
- Tell B to make sure to update once in a day.
- Tell B that each item is updated only once in the system to avoid the same copy of records.

- Tell A that it is not that useful.
- Tell A that it doesn't provide the most recent information because of the update interval time.
- Agree with A and ask him or her if you can adjust the update frequency.
- Tell A that you didn't know that.
- Thank A for the information.

Review expressions

I Match the words (1-8) to the definitions (a-h).

access	1	a	a person employed to look after technical equipment and machines and to repair them if necessary
serial number	2	b	goods that are bought and sold
technician	3	c	the act of helping or assisting someone
noon	4	d	to change something slightly, especially to make it more correct, effective, or suitable
merchandise	5	e	the fact or possibility that you can buy, get, or have something
availability	6	f	a unique sequence of numbers and/or letters used for identification and inventory purposes
adjust	7	g	to open a computer file or to use a computer system such as the Internet
assistance	8	h	twelve o'clock in the middle of the day

II Complete the sentences with the words above.

1 The _____ will arrive by truck at noon.

2 You have to enter a password to _____ the database.

3 The free gift is subject to _____ and change. We ask for your understanding regarding this matter.

4 Your _____ is invalid. Please check it again. It has two letters and four numbers.

5 I'll be happy to provide you with whatever _____ you may need.

6 If the chair is too high you can _____ it to suit you.

7 We don't have in-house _____. After-sales services are provided by third party suppliers.

8 Why don't you go in the morning? The swimming pool doesn't usually get busy until _____.

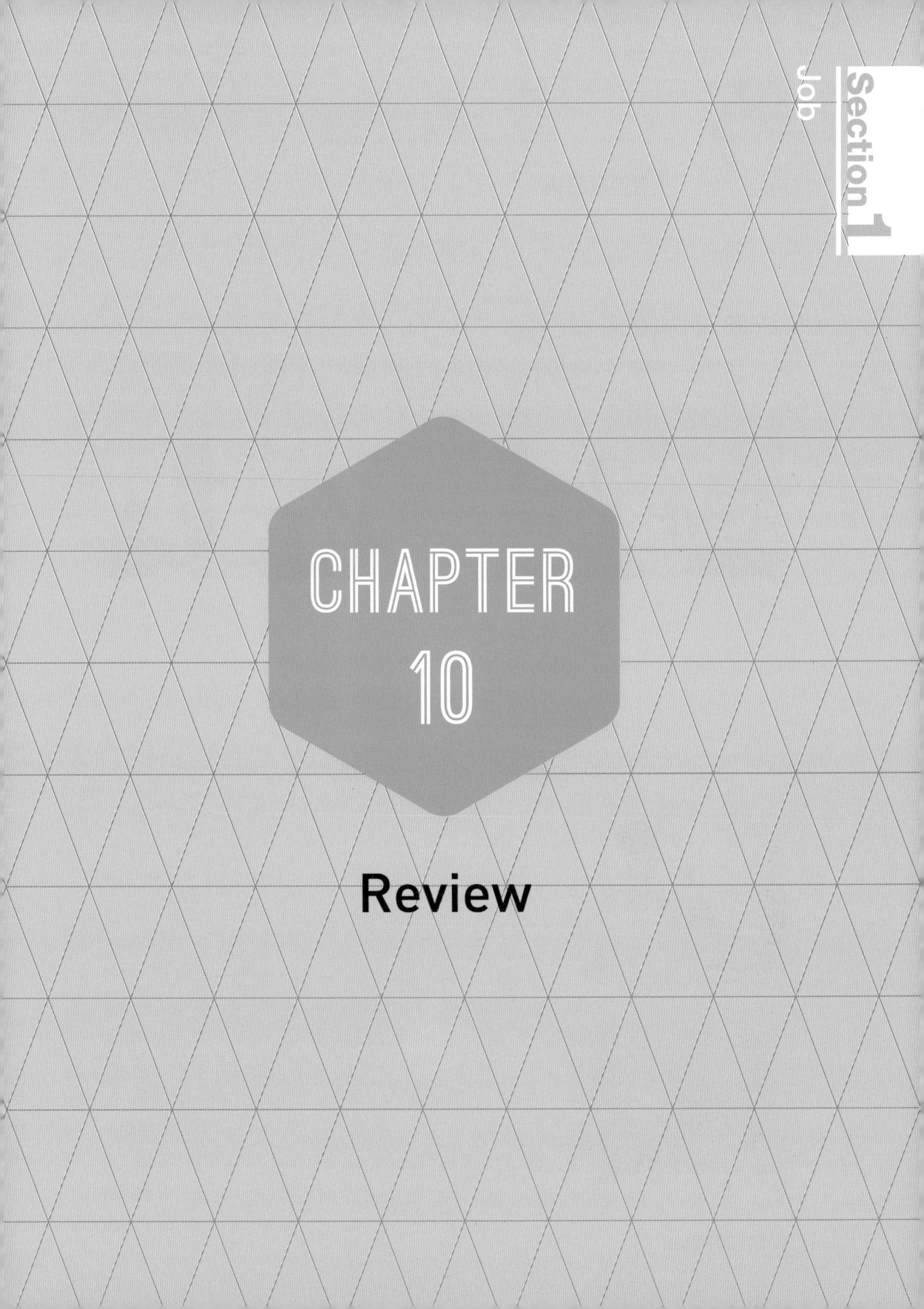

BUSINESS PIONEER

HiEnglish

Review

LISTENING PHOTOGRAPHS

Listen. Then choose the conversation that best describes the photograph.

1

A ☐   B ☐   C ☐   D ☐

2

A ☐   B ☐   C ☐   D ☐

SPEAKING DESCRIBE A PICTURE

Look at the picture for 30 seconds, and then describe it in your own words.

1

2

READING INCOMPLETE SENTENCES

Choose the best word to complete each sentence.

1. The director had a special _____. Our company finally acquired Seiko Corporation, the renowned Japanese software company.

   - ☐ A   information
   - ☐ B   attention
   - ☐ C   announcement
   - ☐ D   guidance

2. My manager would definitely be _____ by recycled materials. We are developing an eco-friendly product.

   - ☐ A   impressed
   - ☐ B   expressed
   - ☐ C   compressed
   - ☐ D   depressed

3. We're out of parts C6 and F78 for model 6527, so I _____ an order.

   - ☐ A   received
   - ☐ B   took
   - ☐ C   finished
   - ☐ D   placed

4. When a customer checks the _____ of an item, the inventory may show that the item is in stock, when in fact it's sold out.

   - ☐ A   possibility
   - ☐ B   availability
   - ☐ C   ability
   - ☐ D   responsibility

5. We apologize again for the _____. Please give me a call if you have any questions.

   - ☐ A   incomplete
   - ☐ B   incorrect
   - ☐ C   inconvenience
   - ☐ D   influence

WRITING WRITE A BUSINESS EMAIL

Write a business email based on the situation below.

> You work in the production team. One of the key materials used in production ran out. You need to ask the purchasing team if the material is available at the moment and request the material be brought down to the production line. Write an email that includes the following:
>
> - You need 1,500 units.
> - The deadline of production is next Friday.
> - If the material is not available, it should be delivered by this week.
> - You need to confirm if this is reported to the Manager of Material Purchase Team.

Section 2 Topic

CHAPTER 11

Company

WARM UP

1. What springs to mind when you hear the word "company?" Is there a particular company you would like to be a part of? Why?

2. Would you prefer to work in a large international company or a small local company? Why?

3. When was the last time you were promoted? Why do you think some people get promoted and others don't?

UNIT 01

Introducing Your Company

HiEnglish

STEP 1 PREPARATION

Sylvia's just heard of Ryan's promotion. She congratulates him now. Listen to the conversation and answer the following questions.

1 What kind of company does Ryan work at?

2 When was Ryan's company founded?

3 How big is Ryan's company?

STEP 2 LISTENING

Listen to the conversation again and fill in as many blanks as you can.

Sylvia	Congratulations! You've _____ _____ again!
Ryan	Thank you so much!
Sylvia	By the way, can you tell me about your company? I've heard of it, but I don't _____ _____ _____ it.
Ryan	My company is the _____ _____ _____ automobile producer. It started in 1967 in Seoul, South Korea.
Sylvia	It has been around for a long time.
Ryan	_____ _____ _____ _____ its foundation, the corporation was very small. Today, we sell vehicles in 193 different countries. And we have about 75,000 employees worldwide.
Sylvia	What about _____ _____ _____? It sounds pretty big.
Ryan	Right. Its revenue is about 76 billion US dollars every year.

64 BUSINESS PIONEER 2

STEP 3 LANGUAGE DEVELOPMENT

Complete the sentences with the right expressions from the box below.

① be promoted
② the world's ... largest
③ automobile producer
④ around for a long time
⑤ the inception of
⑥ sell vehicles
⑦ in ... different countries
⑧ revenue size

1. Let me start off by introducing my company. Feber Insurance is _____ second _____ insurance company.
2. The theater has been _____. It has gone through several owners and remodeling.
3. Although competition was stiff, our _____ grew by 40 percent in the second quarter.
4. As far as customer satisfaction is concerned, we are second to none. MXW is a world renowned _____ providing outstanding service and support.
5. Between you and me, Christina could never have _____ without her team's support.
6. Our company has been _____ in China since 2000. We have a market share of 22 perent.
7. We are one of the major manufacturers of high performance bicycles, bicycle components and related products. We obtained more than 50 patents _____ 20 _____.
8. They have been providing free Wi-Fi service since _____ their business.

STEP 4 ROLE-PLAY

Choose either A or B and have a conversation with your partner according to the directions. Then, switch roles and repeat the conversation.

A
- Congratulate B on his or her promotion.
- Ask B about his or her company.
- Tell B that it has such a long history.
- Ask B about the exports of B's company.
- Ask B about the revenue of B's company.

B
- Thank A.
- Tell A about your company. (Industry and establishment year)
- Tell A more about your company. (The number of employees)
- Tell A about your company's exports. (Exporting countries/markets)
- Tell A about your company's revenue. (Yearly sale)

CHAPTER 11 Company

Unit 02

HiEnglish

Talking About Company System

STEP 1 PREPARATION

Yolanda came across Roy during his morning shift. She's received good news from Roy, which she has been waiting for. Listen to the conversation and answer the following questions.

1 Which shift was Roy supposed to work?

2 What made Roy change his schedule?

3 What was the good news that Yolanda has been waiting for?

STEP 2 LISTENING

Listen to the conversation again and fill in as many blanks as you can.

Yolanda	Hi, Roy. I wasn't expecting you to be here so early. I thought _____ _____ _____ work in the afternoon.
Roy	Well, for the time being, I'll be working the morning shift. The manager _____ _____ _____ another building, so I'm _____ _____ him until our team hires another person.
Yolanda	Really? There's a manager position available on your team? I've been waiting for this kind of opportunity. Do you think I can still _____ _____ _____?
Roy	Sure, but just be aware that you'll be working with many sub-groups.
Yolanda	What do you mean?
Roy	Well, for example, the Public Relations Team works with ours as a sub-roups. If you're okay with that, you'd be _____ _____ _____.
Yolanda	Thank you for the helpful information
Roy	You should hurry though. Interviews start next Monday.

STEP 3 LANGUAGE DEVELOPMENT

Complete the sentences with the right expressions from the box below.

> ① be scheduled to
> ② for the time being
> ③ the morning shift
> ④ get transferred
> ⑤ cover for
> ⑥ submit an application
> ⑦ work with
> ⑧ a good fit

1. Jenna! Have you got a minute to talk? There's a position opening in my department and I think you might be _____.
2. You have no time to waste. You need to _____ in 10 minutes. Have you tried to reboot the computer?
3. I prefer to work _____. I'm not a night person.
4. James is not here anymore. He _____ last month to another branch downtown.
5. I would never _____ my father. I wouldn't even think about it.
6. He's not here _____. He's away on a business trip.
7. I'd like to change my flight to New York, please. It _____ depart at 9:00 a.m. Tuesday this week.
8. Where have you been? You should've told me at least. I had to _____ you.

STEP 4 ROLE-PLAY

Choose either A or B and have a conversation with your partner according to the directions. Then, switch roles and repeat the conversation.

A

- Tell B that you didn't expect to see him or her in the morning.
- Ask B for the reason.
- Ask B if you can apply for the manager position.
- Ask B about sub.groups.
- Thank B for the information.

B

- Tell A that you have to work the morning shift for a while.
- Tell A that your manager got transferred to another team.
- Tell A that he or she needs to consider working with many sub-groups.
- Give A more details. (Your team has some sub-groups such as PR, Marketing Strategy, Maketing Plan, etc.)
- Tell A that interviews start next Monday.

Review expressions

I Match the words (1-8) to the definitions (a-h).

promote	1	a	the income that a business has from its normal business activities, usually from the sale of goods and services to customers.
inception	2	b	to plan or appoint for a certain time or date
foundation	3	c	a period of work in a place such as a factory or hospital
revenue	4	d	an occasion when an organization is established
expect	5	e	the time at which something begins
schedule	6	f	to raise someone to a higher position or rank
shift	7	g	to look forward to the probable occurrence or appearance of
application	8	h	the form or document on which a request is made

II Complete the sentences with the words above.

1. Our firm is looking for another source of _____.
2. Jenny is on the night _____ this month. We rotate it every month.
3. At last, he was _____ to General Manager.
4. Is she _____ you? I haven't heard anything. Please wait here for a moment.
5. Nobody had a positive view on such a scenario at the _____ of the project.
6. Would you fill out this _____ form first? Once it's done, take it to the guy sitting over there.
7. My company was established in 1988. It has continued to prosper since its _____.
8. My favorite prime time soap is _____ to air again in September. I'm so looking forward to it.

Section 2 Topic

CHAPTER 12

Careers & Jobs

WARM UP

1. Can you describe your current job? What's a typical day like?

2. Do you like your job? Why or why not? Do you think it is more important to make a lot of money or to enjoy your job?

3. Have you considered running your own business? What kind of business would you like to run?

Unit 01

Explaining Your Responsibilities

HiEnglish

STEP 1 PREPARATION

Tim met Jackie by chance in front of an elevator. Tim thinks Jackie is a visitor, but she is actually a new employee that just joined the company. Listen to the conversation and answer the following questions.

1. When did Jackie join the company?

2. Which team does Jackie work in?

3. How long has Tim worked in this company?

STEP 2 LISTENING

Listen to the conversation again and fill in as many blanks as you can.

Tim	Hello, do you need any help? Are _____ _____ _____ something?
Jackie	Oh, I'm just waiting for the elevator.
Tim	Do you work here?
Jackie	Yes. My name is Jackie Hwang. I work on video games in the digital design team. I just _____ _____ _____ _____.
Tim	Oh, that's why! My name is Tim Tran. I work in marketing.
Jackie	_____ _____ _____ _____ _____ here?
Tim	Almost five years. But when _____ _____ _____ _____, I was on the product team. One year later, I requested to transfer to the marketing team. There are many _____ _____ _____ between teams at this company.
Jackie	Thanks for the information.

STEP 3 LANGUAGE DEVELOPMENT

Complete the sentences with the right expressions from the box below.

① look for
② be hired
③ work in marketing
④ that's why
⑤ How long have you
⑥ a video game designer
⑦ request to transfer
⑧ opportunities for

1 _____ the barber shop around the corner. You will see a grocery store right across from it.
2 In Korea, I believe women are given fewer _____ career advancement than men.
3 _____ been unemployed? It's really hard to get a job these days, isn't it?
4 I'm going to _____ to another branch in California.
5 I was planning a surprise party! _____ I didn't tell you beforehand.
6 If you _____, it would be your job to plan the best ways to promote your employer's products, services or brand.
7 I know Diane pretty well. We _____ at the same time last year.
8 If you're looking for a profession that combines visual arts and computer programming skills, a job as _____ might be the perfect occupation for you.

STEP 4 ROLE-PLAY

Choose either A or B and have a conversation with your partner according to the directions. Then, switch roles and repeat the conversation.

- Ask B if he or she needs your help.
- Ask B if he or she is an employee.
- Ask B when he or she joined a company.
- Ask B which team he or she works in.
- Answer B's question and wish he or she work good luck.

- Tell A that you're just waiting for the elevator.
- Tell A that you're a new employee.
- Tell A that you joined the company a month ago.
- Answer A's question. Ask A how long A has worked in this company.
- Thank A.

UNIT 02

Current Projects

STEP 1 PREPARATION

Russel and Martha are talking about an ongoing project. Martha appears to have some suggestions. Listen to the conversation and answer the following questions.

1. What is the online servey about?

2. What is Martha waiting for?

3. What does Martha want to do more of? Why?

STEP 2 LISTENING

Listen to the conversation again and fill in as many blanks as you can.

Russel	Hi, Martha. _____ _____ _____ _____ _____? You've just started, right?	
Martha	Right. I'm just waiting for _____ _____ _____ your online survey about the recent changes to our website.	
Russel	Really? John told me that they've already received them. I heard it was mostly _____ _____.	
Martha	Did he? I need to check with him to make sure.	
Russel	They especially liked the interactive features.	
Martha	That's good, but I think we should add more questions to _____ _____ _____ _____.	
Russel	Alright. Do you have any suggestions?	
Martha	Absolutely! I'll _____ _____ _____ _____ before I leave work today.	

STEP 3 LANGUAGE DEVELOPMENT

Complete the sentences with the right expressions from the box below.

> ① How is ... going
> ② work on
> ③ positive feedback
> ④ interactive features
> ⑤ detailed information
> ⑥ any suggestions
> ⑦ get back to
> ⑧ leave work

1. John is a leader who is great at giving _____ to his team members. He knows how to encourage and when to push.
2. I heard you changed jobs. _____ your new job _____?
3. What time do you _____ tomorrow? Let's grab a drink!
4. We are always working to update and improve our products. However, _____ are not supported at the moment.
5. This is a friendly request to participate in an _____ coming to you on Friday. Your help would be greatly appreciated.
6. Although the _____ is correct, I would like to make a few changes if possible.
7. We deeply apologize for the problem you have experienced with your deliveries. I will figure out what happened and _____ you as soon as possible.
8. You can speak freely about this issue. I'll welcome _____.

STEP 4 ROLE-PLAY

Choose either A or B and have a conversation with your partner according to the directions. Then, switch roles and repeat the conversation.

A

- Ask B about an ongoing project.
- Ask B about his or her responsibilities are.
- Tell B that John told you he received most of them.
- Tell B that most of them were positive.
- Suggest that B add additional questions.

B

- Tell A what the project is about. (A survey on recent changes to your company's website)
- Explain to A that you're waiting for the replies to the survey.
- Ask A if he or she knows the results.
- Tell A that you think we should add more questions to get more detailed information.
- Tell A that you will get back to him or her in three hours.

Review expressions

I Match the words (1-8) to the definitions (a-h).

employee	1	a	a person who is responsible for creating all dimensions of a game world.
video game designer	2	b	added or supplementary
hire	3	c	a job that involves encouraging people to buy a product or service
marketing	4	d	an examination of people's opinions or behavior done by asking questions
reply	5	e	a person working for another person or a business firm for pay
survey	6	f	designed to be used in a way that involves the frequent participation of a user
interactive	7	g	to employ someone or pay someone to do a particular job
additional	8	h	a word or a series of words spoken or written in reaction, as to a question or request.

II Complete the sentences with the words above.

1 We need to decide soon what _____ strategy we should pursue for our brand new products.
2 If any _____ needs to take a day off, the person should contact the Personnel Department.
3 Please note that there will be an extra charge for any _____ passengers.
4 Luckily, I was _____ by the first company I applied to.
5 I wonder why there were only a very few _____ to our advertisement.
6 I have a penchant for playing all sorts of games. What education is required to become a _____?
7 A recent _____ showed that more than 60 percent of people do not exercise regularly.
8 Our new _____ displays have attracted many new visitors to the museum.

Section 2 Topic

CHAPTER 13

Colleagues

WARM UP

1. What is the atmosphere like at your workplace? What are the people like? Who's your favorite colleague, and why?

2. Is there anyone you don't get along with? What do you do if you have a problem with a colleague?

3. How important is it to get along with colleagues? Is it a good idea to socialize with them outside work?

UNIT 01

Talking with a New Employee

HiEnglish

STEP 1 PREPARATION

Sally is a new employee who just joined the department. Gerald is her colleague and is asking some questions about her work life. Listen to the conversation and answer the following questions.

1 What does Sally think is best about her job?

2 What is something Sally doesn't like?

3 Why does Geraldi have to leave now?

STEP 2 LISTENING

Listen to the conversation again and fill in as many blanks as you can.

Gerald	How is work _____ _____ _____, Sally? It's been about a month since you started.
Sally	Yes, right. I'm still _____ _____ _____ _____.
Gerald	What do you like best about your job?
Sally	Well, I like meeting people, and I enjoy talking to customers. What about you?
Gerald	My job's interesting, and I like working with the colleagues in my department. They're really nice.
Sally	I absolutely agree with you. But _____ _____ _____ _____ _____ you don't like.
Gerald	Well, I really _____ _____ _____. I'm always so nervous.
Sally	Yeah, me too.
Gerald	Well, I _____ _____, but I should get going. I promised to write a report, and I want to finish it today.
Sally	Okay. Gerald. I _____ _____ _____ _____ at lunch again tomorrow.

76 BUSINESS PIONEER 2

STEP 3 LANGUAGE DEVELOPMENT

Complete the sentences with the right expressions from the box below.

① so far
② It's been about
③ get used to
④ enjoy talking
⑤ like working
⑥ agree with
⑦ give presentations
⑧ write a report

1 I was asked to _____ for the first time. I don't know what to do. Please, help me out.
2 My job involves a lot of travel and overtime work. I didn't like the job much at first but now I'm _____ it.
3 Time really flies, right? So, how do you like living in Germany _____?
4 Do you prefer to work in a team or independently? Honestly, I _____ alone but I'm flexible. So, I can work with the team as well.
5 Since we _____ each other, the matter is settled.
6 Finally, it's time to confirm the contract. _____ a month already.
7 I'm scheduled to _____ three days in a row at the exhibition. I have a lot to prepare.
8 I _____ with her the other day. We have so much in common.

STEP 4 ROLE-PLAY

Choose either A or B and have a conversation with your partner according to the directions. Then, switch roles and repeat the conversation.

A
- Ask B how work is going.
- Ask B what the best thing about his or her work is.
- Answer B's question. Ask B what the worst thing about his or her work is.
- Answer B's question.
- Say goodbye to B.

B
- Answer A.
- Answer A. Ask A the same question.
- Answer A. Ask A the same question.
- Tell A that you need to leave to write a report.
- Say goodbye to A.

Unit 02

Introducing a Colleague

HiEnglish

STEP 1 PREPARATION

Richard is a client of Alana. However, because of a recent event, Alana can't take care of Richard anymore. Listen to the conversation and answer the following questions.

1 What happened to Alana? Why can't she take care of Richard anymore?

2 Who is Amanda?

3 What will Amanda do for Richard?

STEP 2 LISTENING

Listen to the conversation again and fill in as many blanks as you can.

Alana	Hi, Richard, how are you?
Richard	I'm doing well. How have you been doing?
Alana	Very good, thank you. Richard, I _____ _____ _____ _____ another branch office because I had to move with my husband. So, Amanda, my colleague, will _____ _____ _____ _____.
Amanda	Hi, nice to meet you.
Richard	Nice to meet you, too.
Alana	I already showed her _____ _____ _____ _____.
Richard	Do you know when my contract needs to be renewed? Michelle always _____ _____ _____.
Amanda	Sure, I was given all that information.
Richard	Great.
Amanda	Here's my card. If you have any questions, please _____ _____ _____ let me know.

STEP 3 LANGUAGE DEVELOPMENT

Complete the sentences with the right expressions from the box below.

① do well
② apply for
③ transfer to
④ branch office
⑤ take over
⑥ records of purchases
⑦ beforehand
⑧ feel free to

1. There's nothing to worry about. Ms. Lee will _____ my job while I'm on maternity leave.
2. Unemployment compensation is designed to provide income to people who lose their job. Why don't you _____ it?
3. Is she really going to _____ a different department? I thought it's impossible.
4. Don't hesitate to ask anything about the draft. _____ contact me if you have any further questions.
5. Are you really interested? I heard there is a position available in our _____. I can recommend you.
6. Don't worry. I'm sure you'll _____ on the interview.
7. The contact is valid until the end of this month. Let me know _____ if you want to renew the subscription.
8. I want a refund but I've lost the receipt. Do you keep _____?

STEP 4 ROLE-PLAY

Choose either A or B and have a conversation with your partner according to the directions. Then, switch roles and repeat the conversation.

A

- Greet B.
- Tell B that you need to transfer to another branch office.
- Tell B that you have to move with your spouse.
- Tell B that one of your colleagues will take over for you.
- Tell B that you gave all purchase history and information to that person.

B

- Greet A.
- Ask A for the reason.
- Ask A who will replace him or her.
- Ask A if the replacement knows about the renewal of your contract.
- Thank A and ask him or her about the contact information of the replacement.

Review Expressions

I Match the words (1-8) to the definitions (a-h).

department	1	a	an associate in a profession
colleague	2	b	an account or statement describing in detail an event, situation, or the like
presentation	3	c	a local operating division of a business
report	4	d	to make an application or request
apply	5	e	to increase the life of or replace something old
branch	6	f	a part of an organization such as a business, or government that deals with a particular area of work
record	7	g	a talk giving information about something
renew	8	h	a piece of information or a description of an event that is written on paper or stored on a computer

II Complete the sentences with the words above.

1 At the beginning of every year I _____ my membership of the sports club nearby.

2 Obviously, the weather center keeps a _____ of the weather.

3 We're having a small drinks party for one of our _____ who's leaving next week. Would you like to join?

4 If you need more information, you can refer to our company's financial _____.

5 The guest speaker at the expo gave an interesting _____ on future methods of public transportations.

6 I used to work in the local _____ of an Australian National Bank located in northern Sydney.

7 Don't forget to submit your claim for travelling expenses to the accounting _____.

8 By the time I saw the job advertised it was already way too late to _____. What bad luck!

Section 2 Topic

CHAPTER 14

Products

WARM UP

1. What kind of products/service does your company provide? Explain it/them in detail.

2. Why do you buy one product over another?

3. What is the best advertisement you have seen? Did it make you want to buy the product? What makes an ad memorable?

UNIT 01

HiEnglish

Introducing a Product

STEP 1 PREPARATION

Alison is considering purchasing a tablet PC. She is asking Russel about the latest models. Listen to the conversation and answer the following questions.

1 What is the name of the latest product?

2 What are the main features of the new product?

3 Why do you think she says "I need to think about it?"

STEP 2 LISTENING

Listen to the conversation again and fill in as many blanks as you can.

Alison	Can you tell me about your latest tablet PC?
Russel	Yes, of course. You mean the Wide Edge? There are lots of great _____ _____ _____ the Wide Edge. It includes _____ _____ _____ _____ storage and a super high speed processor.
Alison	What about the memory?
Russel	Well, _____ _____ _____ the model. Wide Edge I has 64GB, and the Wide Edge II has 128GB. They are both _____ _____ _____ _____ tablet PCs.
Alison	That's true.
Russel	Old-fashioned tablet PCs had tiny screens, but the Wide Edge has a large 4K screen.
Alison	So, what does _____ _____ _____ _____ ?
Russel	This model, Wide Edge II, costs $99.
Alison	Well, I need to think about it. But thanks for the information.

STEP 3 LANGUAGE DEVELOPMENT

Complete the sentences with the right expressions from the box below.

① latest
② tablet PC
③ new features
④ amount of
⑤ depend on
⑥ bigger than
⑦ old-fashioned
⑧ need to think

1. Our company has a very _____ management structure. Your capabilities don't matter. It's how long you've been with the company that matters.
2. Pear is planning to launch a new _____ called the "M Pad" early next month.
3. It's just perfec for you. You don't _____ about it anymore.
4. The price is negotiable. It _____ the quantity of your order.
5. This new washing machine is big enough for two people. If you buy one that is _____ you need, you'll probably end up running it half-empty more often than not.
6. It was our second stay at the Hilton Hotel. This time, we spent an inordinate _____ time at the pool.
7. I know that Lan and Neige are the _____ products from GDL. Do you know what they are and why they are so special?
8. This model has many _____ for added safety and comfort.

STEP 4 ROLE-PLAY

Choose either A or B and have a conversation with your partner according to the directions. Then, switch roles and repeat the conversation.

A
- Ask B for information on the latest mobile phone.
- Ask B what they are.
- Ask B what the big differences from the previous models are.
- Ask B how much it is.

B
- Explain to A that it has great new features.
- Answer A's question. (Wide screen, design, camera function, etc.)
- Answer A's question.
- Answer A's question.

CHAPTER 14 Products

UNIT 02
Answering to Inquiries of a Product

HiEnglish

STEP 1 PREPARATION

Ben needs to send some documents to Korea ASAP. He needs someone to translate them first. Listen to the conversation and answer the following questions.

1. What are Ben's documents?

2. When is the due date for Ben to send them?

3. Why does Julia say she's not sure of Peter?

STEP 2 LISTENING

Listen to the conversation again and fill in as many blanks as you can.

Ben	I need someone to _____ this contract and instructions _____ _____.
Julia	Let's see …. This is about one of our products, Wide Edge II.
Ben	Right. I need to send them to Korea _____ _____ _____. Is there someone who can do this?
Julia	Well, as you know, most people in the global service team are on vacation. Peter _____ _____ _____, but I'm not sure if he can speak Korean.
Ben	If there is no one, we need to contact a translation service agency.
Julia	Okay. Do you need all parts to be translated? I think we can omit the audio translation function.
Ben	I don't think so. That is _____ _____ _____ _____ _____. Frankly, our previous models were pretty bad.
Julia	Alright. I will ask Peter first _____ _____ _____ _____ this and let you know.

84 BUSINESS PIONEER 2

STEP 3 LANGUAGE DEVELOPMENT

Complete the sentences with the right expressions from the box below.

① translate
② by next Monday
③ as you know
④ on vacation
⑤ on duty
⑥ be not sure if
⑦ frankly
⑧ previous models

1. Could you take a look at this proposal and tell me what you think _____?
2. Alta is said to be more complex than _____. It uses advanced technology to assess your eye health.
3. Emily, would you please _____ the following sentences into Korean for me?
4. Who was _____ last night? The air conditioner was still turned on when I came to the office this morning.
5. I'm leaving _____ to Hawaii tomorrow morning. I'm so looking forward to it.
6. _____ speaking, I forgot her name.
7. I _____ I've told you already. We can provide personalized service.
8. _____, the price of gold is very high these days. We can't accept such a low markdown.

STEP 4 ROLE-PLAY

Choose either A or B and have a conversation with your partner according to the directions. Then, switch roles and repeat the conversation.

A
- Tell B that you need some documents translated into Mandarin.
- Respond to B that they are the contract and MOU.
- Ask B what you can do then.
- Tell B that you need the work done by Friday.
- Tell B that you need them all.

B
- Ask A what the documents are.
- Tell A that you're not sure if there is someone who speaks Mandarin.
- Tell A that you will ask Peter. (But you're not sure about his language ability.)
- Ask A if he or she needs all parts be translated.
- Tell A that you will get them back soon.

Review expressions

I Match the words (1-8) to the definitions (a-h).

latest	1	a	an object or machine that has been invented for a particular purpose
tablet	2	b	to change words into a different language
old-fashioned	3	c	to deal with, have responsibility for, or be in charge of
device	4	d	a small, flat computer that is controlled by touching the screen or by using a special pen
translate	5	e	something that you have to do because it is part of your job
duty	6	f	to fail to include or do something
omit	7	g	not modern; belonging to or typical of a time in the past
handle	8	h	newest or most recent or modern

II Complete the sentences with the words above.

1. I'm not trying to talk behind my boss' back but she is very _____ in her outlook.
2. We enclosed a copy of our _____ brochure, with our compliments.
3. I know it is a difficult passage, but just try to _____ it as best you can.
4. What time are you on _____ tomorrow? Can we still meet at 7pm?
5. We've decided to _____ all the minor details. We're running out of time.
6. If it's a burden for you to _____ the job, I'll get someone else to do it.
7. You are free to stream music either on your tablet or other mobile _____.
8. I don't think I can live without my _____. It's almost a part of my body.

Section 2 Topic

CHAPTER 15

Conflicts

WARM UP

1. What kind of conflicts occur at work? Have you experienced any at your workplace?

2. Have you ever had a conflict with a colleague? Did this affect your performance?

3. What are the best and worst ways to resolve conflicts?

Unit 01

Dealing with Technical Inquiry

HiEnglish

STEP 1 PREPARATION

Eva's production line shut down, so she is asking Ben for help. Ben suggests some solutions. Listen to the conversation and answer the following questions.

1 When is the order date?

2 How does Ben suggest solving the problem?

3 How does Eva suggest solving the problem?

STEP 2 LISTENING

Listen to the conversation again and fill in as many blanks as you can.

Eva	Ben, one of the production lines shut down _____ _____ _____ _____ and is not working now.
Ben	Again? We have to complete XNC's order _____ _____ _____.
Eva	I'm worried that we won't be able to make enough supplies in time.
Ben	You're right. XNC is our biggest client. They don't appreciate delays.
Eva	So, this is not the first time this has happened? What did you do when the machine stopped working before?
Ben	Well, we turned it off, _____ _____ _____ _____ for a while, and then we started it up again. Why don't you try that and _____ _____ _____ _____?
Eva	I've already done that. I think we need to ask the technical support team to identify and _____ _____ _____.
Ben	Okay. I'll contact them myself.

STEP 3 LANGUAGE DEVELOPMENT

Complete the sentences with the right expressions from the box below.

> ① shut down
> ② all of a sudden
> ③ complete one's order
> ④ appreciate delays
> ⑤ stop working
> ⑥ turn off
> ⑦ cool down
> ⑧ troubleshoot problems

1. You're saying that you can deliver it in two weeks but that there will be a 30% increase in delivery cost, right? Okay, we have no choice. The client won't _____.
2. I'm sorry for returning your call so late. I had to attend a meeting _____.
3. There is a problem with your order. Unfortunately, our maximum order size is 2,000 units. So, I don't think our production line can _____.
4. The security system will be _____ over the weekend for routine inspection.
5. Don't forget to _____ all the lights, air-conditioning, and heating equipment on your way out.
6. Can you please send over a technician? The printer just _____ again.
7. There is a handy collection of system utilities included in Windows 10 that can help you _____ that may arise.
8. You need to avoid driving your car until the engine _____.

STEP 4 ROLE-PLAY

Choose either A or B and have a conversation with your partner according to the directions. Then, switch roles and repeat the conversation.

A
- Tell B that one of the production lines shut down suddenly.
- Tell B that it is next Friday.
- Tell B that you did all that.

B
- Ask A when the deadline is.
- Ask A if he or she tried solving the problem. (turn off, cool down, restart)
- Tell A that you will contact technical support.

Unit 02

HiEnglish

Suggesting How to Overcome Conflict

STEP 1 PREPARATION

Sandra looks down. When Scott asks why, Sandra pours out her problems to him. Listen to the conversation and answer the following questions.

1. Who is getting Sandra down?

2. What is the problem Sandra has?

3. What solution does Scott suggest to Sandra?

STEP 2 LISTENING

Listen to the conversation again and fill in as many blanks as you can.

Scott	What's wrong, Sandra? You look rather down.
Sandra	My coworker, Carrie, is _____ _____ _____. She was friendly to me when I first joined the company, but now she's changed.
Scott	Carrie? But she's a really nice person, and she _____ _____ _____ _____ everyone. What has she done to upset you?
Sandra	Well, she's really lazy, and I have to do all the work. She doesn't _____ _____ _____ _____, and my customers get angry.
Scott	Oh dear. That sounds bad.
Sandra	The worst thing is she _____ _____ _____ _____ to the boss.
Scott	Hmm, I think the best solution would be to talk to Carrie. If that doesn't help, you can always _____ _____ _____ _____.
Sandra	Well, that's probably a good idea. I've got an appointment with human resources this afternoon. Keep your fingers crossed for me.

STEP 3 LANGUAGE DEVELOPMENT

Complete the sentences with the right expressions from the box below.

> ① get ... down
> ② join the company
> ③ get along well with
> ④ take down
> ⑤ tell stories about
> ⑥ ask for a transfer
> ⑦ have got an appointment
> ⑧ keep one's fingers crossed

1 Hold on. Let me _____ your name and phone number. I'll make sure to pass it on to Ms. Smith when she comes back.

2 I _____ to see Mr. Edwards at two o'clock. Can I get back to you afterwards?

3 I have no problem adjusting to the new environment. I _____ most of my colleagues, as well.

4 Is it raining again? I really hate the rainy season. It always _____ me _____.

5 She and I _____ at the same time. It's been over a year already.

6 I hesitated because I didn't want to _____ my colleague. I'm usually not that kind of person.

7 This is my third time _____ to an office in France. I'm going to resign if it gets rejected again.

8 Congratulations! That's a good news. I'll _____ for your new business.

STEP 4 ROLE-PLAY

Choose either A or B and have a conversation with your partner according to the directions. Then, switch roles and repeat the conversation.

A

- Tell B he or she looks down.
- Ask B what Rick did. (Rick is very nice to you.)
- Tell B that he or she should talk to Rick directly.
- Tell B that he or she can ask for a transfer.

B

- Explain to A it's because of Rick.
- Tell A what Rick did to you. (Laziness, blaming, neglect, etc.)
- Tell A that you already did so several times.
- Tell A that you will think about it.

Review expressions

I Match the words (1-8) to the definitions (a-h).

sudden	1	a	the answer to a problem
delay	2	b	the division of a company that is focused on providing technical support, advice, and assistance
technical support team	3	c	a fictitious or false statement
troubleshoot	4	d	happening without warning
upset	5	e	the division of a company that is focused on activities relating to employees.
tale	6	f	to make something happen at a later time than originally planned or expected
solution	7	g	to locate the cause of a problem and remove or treat it
human resources department	8	h	to make someone worried, unhappy, or angry

II Complete the sentences with the words above.

1. Our company recently added hundreds of workers to _____ the new machines.
2. Don't say there's no easy _____ to this problem. You must figure it out.
3. Don't _____ yourself over it. It's not too late to start over.
4. When you have a problem with another co-worker, you should talk to _____ so they can file the issue and go through any a particular process to handle the complaint.
5. Would it be possible to postpone our meeting until five? My plane is _____ by an hour.
6. Don't tell her anything personal. She's such a big mouth and is the sort of person who is always telling _____ about other people.
7. Equipped with technical expertise and background, our _____ is ready to assist customers on proper techniques and best practices.
8. She got promoted all of a _____. It came as a total surprise to all of us.

Section 2 Topic

CHAPTER 16

Collaboration & Cooperation

WARM UP

1. What types of jobs require high or low degrees of teamwork?

2. Do you have a job that requires a lot of teamwork?

3. What is a polite way to request assistance from other co-workers?

HiEnglish

Distributing Responsibilities

STEP 1 PREPARATION

Nick, Emily, and Ashley are preparing to receive visitors. Listen to the conversation and answer the following questions

1. What did Emily confirm?

2. What was the next agenda item they need to decide on?

3. Who will take a responsibility for finding a restaurant?

STEP 2 LISTENING

Listen to the conversation again and fill in as many blanks as you can.

Nick	Okay, the visitors will arrive on Monday afternoon, and it's our job to take care of the Taiwanese group and _____ _____ _____ _____. Emily, have you reserved the hotel rooms yet?
Emily	Yes, they're confirmed. I've already sent you the email.
Nick	Good, thanks. Now on Monday evening we'll have dinner together. We'll _____ _____ _____ to a nice restaurant so that we can get to know each other. Any restaurant ideas?
Asheley	I think we should take them somewhere where they serve _____ _____ _____. Have you been to Hankook House, the new traditional Korean food restaurant in Bukchon Hanok Village yet?
Nick	No, I've heard about it though. Isn't it expensive?
Asheley	I haven't tried it either but I don't think it's too expensive. The food will be good, and the area is interesting for visitors, too.
Nick	That sounds good. Could you check out _____ _____ _____ _____ _____ too?
Asheley	Will do.

STEP 3 LANGUAGE DEVELOPMENT

Complete the sentences with the right expressions from the box below.

① take care of
② feel welcome
③ have dinner together
④ take A out to B
⑤ get to know
⑥ somewhere
⑦ traditional Korean food
⑧ a couple of

1   I moved from the countryside three years ago. It took a while for me to _____ the city properly.
2   I don't want to go _____ where there's Wi-Fi.
3   Thank you so much! People here are very friendly and have made me _____.
4   Of course. I'll send you a report about the damage. I'll _____ it first thing tomorrow.
5   Our family _____ at least twice a week. I need to get going now.
6   I'm a part-timer. I only work here _____ hours a week.
7   David is having a hard time. He's stuck in his room. Let's _____ him _____ a restaurant for dinner. He needs to get some fresh air.
8   Have you tried any of _____ during your stay? How did you like it?

STEP 4 ROLE-PLAY

Choose either A or B and have a conversation with your partner according to the directions. Then, switch roles and repeat the conversation.

- Ask B when the visitors will arrive.
- Ask B which restaurant you can take them out to for dinner.
- Ask B if it's expensive.
- Ask B if he or she has been there.
- Tell B it sounds good. Then ask B to check out a couple of other places.

- Tell A that they'll arrive on Monday.
- Tell A that you know a traditional Korean restaurant. (Describe the restaurant.)
- Tell A you don't think so.
- Tell A that you haven't yet, but you've heard good things.
- Agree with A.

CHAPTER 16 Collaboration & Cooperation

UNIT 02

HiEnglish

Requesting for Cooperation

STEP 1 PREPARATION

Jeffrey is asking Michelle to help him out. Listen to the conversation and answer the following questions.

1 What did Jeffrey ask Michelle?

2 How did Michelle respond to Jeffery?

3 Do you think Jeffrey is fully prepared?

STEP 2 LISTENING

Listen to the conversation again and fill in as many blanks as you can.

Jeffrey	Good morning, Michelle. I submitted next year's budget request for my department, but I was wondering if you could _____ _____ _____ for me.
Michelle	Well, _____ _____ _____ requests was yesterday, but the financial director won't review them until tomorrow morning, so I should be able to help you.
Jeffrey	That's great. I want to _____ the data software program in the list _____ a different one. It's a bit more expensive, but it will absolutely be more useful for my department's work.
Michelle	I've thought about your request, and since it's just one item, it won't be a problem.
Jeffrey	Thanks, I'm glad _____ _____ _____.
Michelle	Just let me know what the cost difference is, and I'll make the change now.
Jeffrey	Here is the final figure. Do you think I need to _____ _____?
Michelle	I think the director will definitely want to look at it.

96 BUSINESS PIONEER 2

STEP 3 LANGUAGE DEVELOPMENT

Complete the sentences with the right expressions from the box below.

① budget request
② I was wondering if
③ make changes
④ the deadline for
⑤ financial director
⑥ replace A with B
⑦ be a problem
⑧ final figure

1. The government today released details of the president's _____ for the 2017 fiscal year.
2. All employees are required to _____ their existing ID cards _____ a new one by the end of this month.
3. _____ we can make a two-year contract and extend it every two years.
4. A new _____ has been appointed one week after firing the previous one.
5. Once it's signed, you cannot _____. Are we clear?
6. That wouldn't _____. Our company handles a lot of overseas customers.
7. You can't apply anymore. _____ applications has expired.
8. We can knock 15% off the price if you order over 1,000 units. This is the _____ we can give you.

STEP 4 ROLE-PLAY

Choose either A or B and have a conversation with your partner according to the directions. Then, switch roles and repeat the conversation.

A
- Tell B that you submitted the report, but you have some things to change.
- Tell B that you want B to replace some figures on the expense sheet.
- Explain to B that those programs are really useful for your department's work.
- Thank B for that and ask B if you need to attach estimates.

B
- Tell A that the deadline is tomorrow, so that's possible.
- Tell A that you will do so, but that some figures look a bit high.
- Tell A that you approve and that you've changed the figures.
- Tell A that it's better for the director because he or she might want to look at it.

Review expressions

I Match the words (1-8) to the definitions (a-h).

welcome	1	a	to make an arrangement, plan, or meeting certain or fixed
confirm	2	b	an area of a country or town that has a particular feature that makes it different from surrounding areas
traditional	3	c	the symbol for a number or an amount expressed in numbers
deadline	4	d	a statement for a possible customer about how much a piece of work should cost
district	5	e	following or belonging to the ways of behaving or beliefs that have been established for a long time
approve	6	f	a time or day by which something must be done
figure	7	g	to meet and speak to someone in a friendly way when they arrive
estimate	8	h	to have a positive opinion of someone or something

II Complete the sentences with the words above.

1 Can you read this _____? Is it a three or an eight?

2 If it is discovered that the cost will be greater than originally estimated, a revised _____ may then be sent to you.

3 I was warmly _____ by the head of the department.

4 Can you name one of the Korean _____ musical instruments for me?

5 Hello, this is Amy Hens from ABC Inc. I'm calling to _____ our appointment next Monday.

6 The theater _____ in New York is in midtown Manhattan. It's my dream to watch a musical there.

7 It's already Wednesday. There's no way I can meet that _____.

8 I thought my boss didn't _____ my request to take a month's paid leave.

Section 2 Topic

CHAPTER 17

Culture

WARM UP

1. What is the ideal company culture for you? What type of work environment do you prefer?

2. What do you normally wear to work? Does your company have a strict dress code?

3. What's one thing you would change about your company if you could?

Unit 01

HiEnglish

Company Dress Code

STEP 1 PREPARATION

Will looks more casual than usual today. Jessica is wondering why. Listen to the conversation and answer the following questions.

1. Why does Will wear casual clothes?

2. What does carbon footprint mean in this conversation? Have you heard of it before?

3. What is the relationship between casual clothes and one's carbon footprint?

STEP 2 LISTENING

Listen to the conversation again and fill in as many blanks as you can.

Jessica	You're dressed quite casual. Haven't you been to work today?
Will	Yes, I have. This is our _____ _____ _____ _____. We don't have to wear formal clothes anymore.
Jessica	Why did your company change the dress code _____ _____ _____ _____?
Will	We are _____ _____ _____ _____ and saving energy by setting the air conditioner a little higher.
Jessica	And who came up with that idea?
Will	Ms. Martinez, my boss. She calculated the company's _____ _____ and was extremely shocked.
Jessica	I know about carbon footprints, but I've never checked mine. What was the result?
Will	It was huge. She says if we don't all become more _____ _____, we'll destroy the planet.

100 BUSINESS PIONEER 2

STEP 3 LANGUAGE DEVELOPMENT

Complete the sentences with the right expressions from the box below.

① office dress code
② formal clothes
③ cooling costs
④ save energy
⑤ come up with
⑥ carbon footprint
⑦ environmentally friendly
⑧ destroy the planet

1. Let's _____ for the planet. It's more important than you know.
2. No matter your _____, these are some do's and don'ts that hold true for everyone.
3. Everyone's _____ is different depending on their location, habits, and personal choices.
4. Really? Is that the best you can _____?
5. Being _____ simply means having a lifestyle that is better for the environment.
6. We shouldn't overlook global warming and climate change. This may _____ eventually.
7. In the summer, many people turn on the air conditioner. This new technology can reduce _____ by as much as 50 percent.
8. You need to wear _____ to the event this Thursday. Wearing a tie is a must.

STEP 4 ROLE-PLAY

Choose either A or B and have a conversation with your partner according to the directions. Then, switch roles and repeat the conversation.

A
- Tell B that he or she looks very casual today.
- Ask B why it was changed all of a sudden.
- Ask B whose idea it was.
- Ask B what made him or her suggest this idea.
- Ask B what the result was.

B
- Tell A that this is your new office dress code.
- Tell A that it helps keep cooling costs down.
- Tell A that it was your boss's.
- Tell A she calculated the company's carbon footprint one day and was shocked.
- Tell A that it was huge.

UNIT 02

HiEnglish

Discussing a Business Motto

STEP 1 PREPARATION

Mia is sharing an embarrassing memory of a meeting. She and Chen are talking about their company motto. Listen to the conversation and answer the following questions.

1 Why was Mia embarrassed in the staff meeting?

2 What is the business motto?

3 Where did Mia and Chen first learn about the company motto?

STEP 2 LISTENING

Listen to the conversation again and fill in as many blanks as you can.

Mia	Hi, Chen. Do you remember the _____ _____ of our company? A board member asked me all of a sudden in a staff meeting, but my mind went blank.
Chen	Oh, you must have been so embarrassed. The motto is "_____ & _____." I heard the founder wanted to motivate employees with this motto.
Mia	That's right! Why couldn't I remember such a short phrase?
Chen	I think it was introduced during the _____ _____ _____.
Mia	You're right! I remember now. That was a part of the _____ _____.
Chen	This is why orientation is important. New employees _____ _____ _____ about the company.
Mia	I absolutely agree! Remember Mr. Levinson's speech? All the new employees _____ _____ _____ work hard.

STEP 3 LANGUAGE DEVELOPMENT

Complete the sentences with the right expressions from the box below.

① business motto
② go blank
③ founder
④ new employee orientation
⑤ a part of
⑥ such a
⑦ required training
⑧ be inspired to

1. The company will provide _____ to production line staff about assembling different components to increase productivity.
2. I don't understand why he pays attention to _____ trivial thing.
3. I _____ share these key tips with you because I also have gone through stages in my career where I had no direction or confidence.
4. All new employees are required to attend _____ within the first 30 days.
5. I was so nervous during the interview that when I was asked about my experience, my mind _____ .
6. Honeycell was born in the summer of 2013. Back then, the _____ had no idea what the company would become.
7. Customer satisfaction is our _____ and we aim for 100% customer satisfaction.
8. No offense but I don't want you to be _____ that.

STEP 4 ROLE-PLAY

Choose either A or B and have a conversation with your partner according to the directions. Then, switch roles and repeat the conversation.

A

- Tell B that you were asked a question you couldn't answer in a meeting this morning.
- Ask B if he or she remembers the company motto.
- Ask B when he or she learned it.
- Agree to B's opinion and tell B that you remember now .

B

- Console A.
- Answer A with your company's motto.
- Explain to A that you learned it during orientation.
- Tell A that the orientation is a very important step for new employees.

CHAPTER 17 Culture 103

Review expressions

I Match the words (1-8) to the definitions (a-h).

dress code	1	a	the amount of carbon dioxide released into the atmosphere as a result of the activities of a particular individual or organization
calculate	2	b	someone who establishes an organization
carbon footprint	3	c	a set of rules or guidelines regarding the manner of dress acceptable in an office, restaurant, etc
planet	4	d	to fill someone with confidence and desire to do something
motto	5	e	to determine by mathematical methods
founder	6	f	a short sentence or phrase that expresses a belief or purpose
orientation	7	g	an extremely large, round mass of rock and metal, or of gas, that moves in a circular path around the sun or another star
inspire	8	h	training or preparation for a new job or activity

II Complete the sentences with the words above.

1 We all need to look for ways to reduce our _____.
2 Do you want to know what my _____ is? It's "Always do my best"
3 I'm trying to _____ how long the project will take to complete.
4 Dr Kim's speech was really amazing, wasn't it? I was _____ by her words, too.
5 Is it too late to repair the damage we have done to our_____?
6 My company doesn't really have a _____. I can even wear shorts to work.
7 You will be given an _____ before your project starts.
8 Dominic Cha is the _____ and managing director of my company.

Section 2 Topic

CHAPTER 18

Business Communication

WARM UP

1. Have you ever participated in a videoconference? Is it more or less difficult than a face-to-face meeting?

2. What are the pros and cons of videoconferencing? Can you think of any problems that may arise? How can they be overcome?

3. What are some things posted on your company's bulletin board? Have you ever posted something on it? What was it?

Unit 01

HiEnglish

Videoconferencing

STEP 1 PREPARATION

Alison and Joe are having a videoconference this afternoon. Listen to the conversation and answer the following questions.

1 What is Joe responsible for?

2 Why is Joe so nervous about this afternoon videoconference?

3 Why does Alison think videoconferencing is important to her work?

STEP 2 LISTENING

Listen to the conversation again and fill in as many blanks as you can.

Alison	Hi, Joe. Are you attending the videoconference this afternoon?
Joe	I have to be there. I'm responsible for _____ _____ _____ _____, and I'm a bit nervous about it.
Alison	Oh? Why?
Joe	Remember _____ _____ _____ we had a videoconference? We had to stop _____ _____ _____ _____.
Alison	Yes, I remember. I can see why you're nervous, but I'm sure it _____ _____ _____.
Joe	Videoconferences are just so important for our work.
Alison	Of course. They're perfect for _____ _____ _____ _____ our business partners.
Joe	Right. We have _____ _____ all over the world. We save time and transportation costs by videoconferencing.

106 BUSINESS PIONEER 2

STEP 3 LANGUAGE DEVELOPMENT

Complete the sentences with the right expressions from the box below.

> ① videoconference
> ② be responsible for
> ③ set up the equipment
> ④ the last time
> ⑤ technical issues
> ⑥ keep in touch with
> ⑦ business contacts
> ⑧ all over the world

1. Our company now delivers _____. We offer free International Delivery on all orders over $70.
2. My name is Chris Hanson, and I _____ the International Sales Department at KBM Korea.
3. Do you know how to _____ for a PowerPoint presentation in room 202?
4. Think back to _____ we sold as many as 5,000 printers. That number will soar if we spend more money on marketing.
5. Oh, I see. You are going on a business trip that day. Would you like me to arrange a _____ instead?
6. The event will be such a great opportunity for us to meet other potential _____.
7. Do you remember Jason who left our company last May? Do you still _____ him?
8. I'm happy to help with any _____. If they arise, don't hesitate to ask me.

STEP 4 ROLE-PLAY

Choose either A or B and have a conversation with your partner according to the directions. Then, switch roles and repeat the conversation.

A
- Ask B if he or she is attending the video conference this afternoon.
- Tell B that he/she looks nervous.
- Tell B those problems won't happen.
- Tell B you agree because it is perfect for keeping in touch with business partners.
- Tell B that you can save the time and costs thanks to videoconferencing.

B
- Tell A that you have to be there because you're responsible for setting up the quipment.
- Tell A that you are because of problems that might occur during the videoconference.
- Tell A that you think videoconferencing is important for your work.
- Tell A he or she is right because your company has business contacts all over the world.

Unit 02

HiEnglish

In-company Bulletin Boards

STEP 1 PREPARATION

Tanaka brings up an article she read about their company, but Alison hasn't read it. Listen to the conversation and answer the following questions.

1. What was the article about?

2. How does Alison suggest sharing the article with other employees?

3. Why does Alison suggest that idea?

STEP 2 LISTENING

Listen to the conversation again and fill in as many blanks as you can.

Tanaka	Hi, Alison. Have you seen the website of Business World? There is an article that says we're _____ _____ _____ mobile phone company in the country.
Alison	Oh, really? I haven't read it yet.
Tanaka	It's _____ _____ _____ _____ _____ on their site.
Alison	Why don't you _____ _____ _____ _____ _____ on the company bullentin board?
Tanaka	Good idea. Media coverage will make employees _____ _____ in the company and what they do.
Alison	It will definitely help our recruiting campaign.
Tanaka	That's right! It will certainly attract _____ _____ _____ _____ to our company.
Alison	You'd _____ _____ _____ to your computer and add the link right now!

STEP 3 LANGUAGE DEVELOPMENT

Complete the sentences with the right expressions from the box below.

① one of the top stories
② the fastest growing
③ post a link
④ media coverage
⑤ feel pride
⑥ recruiting campaign
⑦ job applicants
⑧ go off

1 Sorry, I have to _____ to my office and finish the report.
2 Luckily, our bus campaign received extensive _____.
3 I tried to _____ to YouMovie the other night but it didn't work.
4 _____ must show they meet the requirements of the position.
5 I would love the opportunity to work at _____ technology company in Korea.
6 Our company is running a _____ at the moment. Please visit the job openings page on our website.
7 I've just read the article about cell phone addiction you told me about. It was _____ in the news.
8 When you do a good job or finish a difficult task, you _____.

STEP 4 ROLE-PLAY

Choose either A or B and have a conversation with your partner according to the directions. Then, switch roles and repeat the conversation.

A
- Ask B if he or she saw the Business World website.
- Tell B that an article about your company was one of the top stories.
- Ask B why he or she wants you to do that.
- Agree with B and add that the article might make employees feel pride in the company and what they do.
- Agree with B.

B
- Tell A that you haven't yet.
- Ask A if he or she can post a link to it on your company website.
- Tell A that it can direct employees to the article.
- Tell B that it will also help your campaign to recruit new employees.
- Tell B to go to the computer right now and add the link.

REVIEW EXPRESSIONS

I Match the words (1-8) to the definitions (a-h).

videoconference	1	a	the reporting of a particular important event or subject
responsible	2	b	a feeling of happiness that you get when you or someone you know does something good, difficult, etc.
equipment	3	c	likely to be or become something specified in the future
accommodations	4	d	the holding of a conference among people at remote locations by means of transmitted audio and video signals
coverage	5	e	a place (such as a room in a hotel) where travelers can sleep and find other services
pride	6	f	having to do something as your duty
recruit	7	g	supplies or tools needed for a special purpose
prospective	8	h	to employ new people to work for a company or organization

II Complete the sentences with the words above.

1 Sally is the HR manager of our company. She is _____ for the education of new employees.
2 All of the medical _____ must be sterilized before use under the current law.
3 The agency we contacted wasn't sure if they could provide food and _____ for 300 people.
4 It is likely that the use of _____ will continue to increase over the next few years.
5 The careers fair gives students a chance to meet _____ employers.
6 That case received heavy _____ in the mass media.
7 You should take more _____ in your work.
8 The ANC shopping center is _____ extra staff for the Christmas period.

110 BUSINESS PIONEER 2

Section 2 Topic

CHAPTER 19

Achievement

WARM UP

1. What is your greatest accomplishment at your current/last job?

2. Have you ever been promoted? What kind of benefits did you get? How did you feel?

3. Where do you see yourself five years from now? Be specific.

UNIT 01

HiEnglish

Recognition

STEP 1 PREPARATION

Jess is talking about a highly-skilled engineer. Harry's letting her know what she should do. Listen to the conversation and answer the following questions.

1. Why is the engineer recognized by the company?

2. What is the engineer going to do?

3. What is the first thing that Jess should do?

STEP 2 LISTENING

Listen to the conversation again and fill in as many blanks as you can.

Jess	Harry, I've got some great news. Jim Campbell, the program engineer, just told me that he can _____ _____ _____ for our firm's employees the third week of this month.
Harry	That's good to hear. I understand that many companies want him as a programmer, so I'm happy that we _____ _____ _____ _____ him.
Jess	What should we do then?
Harry	We must _____ _____ _____ of individuals attending so that we can make sure our room is _____ _____.
Jess	Should I send an _____ _____ to all employees?
Harry	Well, I guess you can email the department managers and ask them how many people will be going to the workshop.
Jess	That would be faster. I'll handle that.

112 BUSINESS PIONEER 2

STEP 3 LANGUAGE DEVELOPMENT

Complete the sentences with the right expressions from the box below.

① program engineer
② hold a workshop
③ be able to book
④ the number of
⑤ send an email invitation
⑥ large enough
⑦ so that we can
⑧ department managers

1. Why don't we _____ instead? It will save time and money.
2. We will _____ on "Digital Transportation" on May 11th in our conference room. This workshop will bring together several leading experts in telecommunications.
3. BLC mart is raising wages for _____ and workers in its deli and other specialized departments.
4. We are currently looking for a _____ who has experience with 3D CAD software, preferably Denseworks.
5. With this application, you'll _____ discounted last-minute hotel rooms right from your phone.
6. _____ sales was huge last year. We have recorded the biggest annual profit in corporate history.
7. Explain what is going on _____ understand.
8. I'd like to purchase a suitcase. It should be _____ to hold a B4 sized folder. Do you have one in stock?

STEP 4 ROLE-PLAY

Choose either A or B and have a conversation with your partner according to the directions. Then, switch roles and repeat the conversation.

A
- Tell B that Jim Campbell's been offered a speaking gig at your company.
- Tell B that you didn't know Jim is so capable.
- Ask B what you need to do.
- Ask B if you should send an email invitation to all employees.
- Agree with B because it would be faster.

B
- Tell A that you understand and explain why Jim is in demand from many companies.
- Tell A that you are lucky to book him for the company workshop.
- Tell A he or she needs to verify how many people are planning to attend Jim's workshop and tell A why.
- Tell A to email department managers only.

CHAPTER 19 Achievement

UNIT 02

HiEnglish

Getting a Promotion

STEP 1 PREPARATION

Tammy congratulates Ben on his promotion. And Tammy is talking about what Ben's done so far. Listen to the conversation and answer the following questions.

1. What did Ben do before his promotion?

2. Where did Ben work for ten years?

3. What will Ben share in his training sessions?

STEP 2 LISTENING

Listen to the conversation again and fill in as many blanks as you can.

Tammy	Congratulations on your promotion, Ben. We'll certainly miss _____ _____ _____ the sales staff.
Ben	Thanks, Tammy.
Tammy	I know you'll be an excellent corporate trainer. I understand you've already prepared a series of training sessions on sales strategies.
Ben	That's right. I've been selling furniture for about ten years now in this store, and I have a lot of _____ _____ _____ that I would like to share.
Tammy	What are some things you want to share?
Ben	You know, things like _____ _____ with customers, communicating effectively, handling complaints, and so on.
Tammy	I've seen you _____ _____ _____ many times. We can all _____ _____ _____ _____. When is your first session going to be?
Ben	In just three weeks, on July 21. I hope _____ _____ _____ _____.

STEP 3 LANGUAGE DEVELOPMENT

Complete the sentences with the right expressions from the box below.

> ① congratulations on
> ② a series of
> ③ training sessions
> ④ establish trust
> ⑤ communicate effectively
> ⑥ handle complaints
> ⑦ interact with
> ⑧ in just three weeks

1 How should I _____ effectively? I never get used to them.
2 Korea's largest shopping mall multiplex has attracted over 3 million visitors _____ of its opening.
3 I hope time stops right now. _____ meetings are waiting for me next week.
4 I get along well with all of my co-workers. I enjoy _____ people a lot.
5 Several _____ will take place in two weeks. These sessions are designed for new or less experienced workers in RCO Inc.
6 _____ winning the Employee of the Year Award. I am so proud that someone from my department won, and I am happy that it was you.
7 The first thing you need to do is _____ with him. Don't expect too much too soon. Focus on small steps and small commitments.
8 Our employees are expected to be able to _____ in English.

STEP 4 ROLE-PLAY

Choose either A or B and have a conversation with your partner according to the directions. Then, switch roles and repeat the conversation.

A
- Congratulate B on his or her promotion.
- Tell B that you expect B will be an excellent corporate trainer.
- Ask B what he or she wants to share.
- Ask B for some details.
- Ask B when the session is.

B
- Thank A.
- Thank A again and tell him or her that you have so many experiences to share.
- Tell A that it's about effective sales methods.
- Tell A that it would be some things like establishing trust, communicating effectively, handling complaints, and so on.
- Tell A that it will be in three weeks and you hope A can make it.

Review expressions

I Match the words (1-8) to the definitions (a-h).

workshop	1	a	a detailed plan for achieving success in situations
book	2	b	a statement that something is wrong or not satisfactory
verify	3	c	a meeting of people to discuss and/or perform practical work in a subject or activity
invitation	4	d	to check or prove that something is correct or true
promotion	5	e	to arrange to have a seat, room, performer, etc. at a particular time in the future
corporate trainer	6	f	an instructor who works in a business environment and conveys knowledge or skills to a group of employees
strategy	7	g	a written or spoken request to come somewhere or do something, or the act of inviting someone
complaint	8	h	the advancement of someone to a more important rank or position

II Complete the sentences with the words above.

1 We had a salary dispute. I worked for them as a _____ for five years and never got a raise.

2 We've received lots of _____ about our renewed program. What is our plan of action?

3 A _____ about leadership will be held in Room 201. Dr. Murphy Robinson is the guest speaker.

4 I've _____ a table for three at the Japanese restaurant for six o'clock tomorrow.

5 Please _____ your credit card information and try again.

6 Our wedding is around the corner. We need to send out our wedding _____ before it's too late.

7 It's important to continually reevaluate your sales _____ with your staff.

8 Tony was recommended for _____ by his manager this time.

Section 2 Topic

CHAPTER 20

Review

BUSINESS PIONEER

HiEnglish

Review

LISTENING PHOTOGRAPHS

Listen. Then choose the conversation that best describes the photograph.

1

A ☐ B ☐ C ☐ D ☐

2

A ☐ B ☐ C ☐ D ☐

SPEAKING DESCRIBE A PICTURE

Look at the picture for 30 seconds, and then describe it in your own words.

1

2

READING INCOMPLETE SENTENCES

Choose the best word to compete each sentence.

1 At the _____ of its foundation, the corporation was very small. Today, we sell vehicles in 193 different countries. And we have about 75,000 employees worldwide.

- ☐ A application
- ☐ B inception
- ☐ C concept
- ☐ D perception

2 Richard, I applied for _____ to another branch office because I had to move with my husband.

- ☐ A transfer
- ☐ B transaction
- ☐ C transportation
- ☐ D translation

3 There are lots of great new features in the Wide Edge. It includes a(n) _____ amount of storage and a super high speed processor.

- ☐ A entire
- ☐ B anonymous
- ☐ C unanimous
- ☐ D enormous

4 Well, as you know, most people in the global service team are on vacation. Peter is on _____, but I'm not sure if he can speak Korean.

- ☐ A task
- ☐ B responsibility
- ☐ C duty
- ☐ D assignment

5 Remember Mr. Levinson's speech? All the new employees were _____ to work hard.

- ☐ A inspired
- ☐ B expired
- ☐ C conspired
- ☐ D aspired

CHAPTER 20 Review

WRITING WRITE A BUSINESS EMAIL

Write a business email based on the situation below.

> You are on the sales team. One of your clients requested information on the features and functions of a new product your company just released. You don't much know about it, so you need to get that information from the R&D team. Write a polite email that includes requests for the following :
>
> - Key features for users
> - New functions added to the new product
> - Availability of brochure for the product

Answer Key

HiEnglish

CHAPTER 01 Human Resources

UNIT 01

STEP 2 LISTENING

Jeff So after the final round of interviews, two candidates, Diane and Andrew, really stand out.
Sophia I agree. Well, between Diane and Andrew, who strikes you as the better candidate?
Jeff It's a tough one. The both are very qualified.
Sophia Right. Well, what we really need is a smart person who will fit well with our organization.
Jeff Yes, Diane is probably a better overall match. I think her dynamic style aligns well with our organizational culture.
Sophia Then, what's holding you back?
Jeff Well, the main issue I'm worried about is compensation. Her salary history suggests she wants something on the high end of our range.
Sophia Well, let's give her an offer and see how she reacts. In the meantime we can keep Andrew on the back burner.
Jeff That's exactly what I was thinking.

STEP 3 LANGUAGE DEVELOPMENT

1. fit well with   2. on the back burner   3. stand out
4. In the meantime   5. candidates   6. held back
7. That's exactly   8. compensation

UNIT 02

STEP 2 LISTENING

Dylan So Andrea, tell us a little bit about your job as a training manager.
Andrea Well, basically, I'm responsible for the effective planning and execution of training and development programs for the whole company.
Dylan I see. And what exactly does that entail?
Andrea Quite a lot, actually. Let's see ... I consider the developmental needs in order to drive training initiatives. I also identify the range suitable training solutions for employees. This means I need to design and implement all aspect of the training programs to educate people on standard processes and to enhance performance according to the needs of the company.
Dylan And what kind of programs do you run?
Andrea We run the full gamut really – quality control, work measurement, human resources, manufacturing methods, development of supervisors, you name it.
Dylan Okay. Can you tell us more about some of your specific duties?
Andrea Sure. For example, I oversee the development of training content including formulating and reviewing course outlines.

STEP 3 LANGUAGE DEVELOPMENT

1. execution   2. responsible for   3. oversee
4. enhanced   5. according to   6. Basically
7. you name it   8. quality control

REVIEW EXPRESSIONS

I   1. c 2. h 3. a 4. g 5. f 6. b 7. d 8. e
II 1. formulating 2. supervisor 3. performance 4. fit
    5. entail 6. initiatives 7. gamut 8. qualified

CHAPTER 02 Finance & Accounting

UNIT 01

STEP 2 LISTENING

Mike Today, we're going to discuss our targets for first half profits. Treestar is still our largest client by far. We need to keep taking good care of them, of course.
Shelly But we can't just depend on them. What happens if they leave us?
Emily Shelly is right. We need to concentrate on getting more business from smaller clients so that we remain stable even if we lose Treestar.
Mike How do you suggest we do that, Emily?
Emily I guess the first thing we need to do is to look into what cases we've handled for other clients and how much money we made from each.

Mike	Does everyone know how to do that?
Emily	I can email all of you a file that <u>contains detailed information on</u> how to write the report if you want.
Mike	That would be great.

STEP 3 LANGUAGE DEVELOPMENT
1. detailed information
2. concentrating on
3. wrote the report
4. take good care of
5. by far
6. remain stable
7. Even if
8. looking into

UNIT 02
STEP 2 LISTENING

Gabriella	Excuse me, Ito. Since you're our department's manager, I was hoping I could <u>get your approval</u> to use three of my vacation days at the start of December.
Ito	Sure, but how is the fiscal year report you've been working on? The deadline is getting closer.
Gabriella	I've already completed <u>my portion of</u> it. I can send you the final draft by tomorrow morning.
Ito	That's good to hear. But there are still a few more tasks that must be finished before the end of the month, and I'm worried that the report <u>won't be completed on time</u> without you.
Gabriella	That won't be an issue. I'm willing to <u>take on extra work</u> and finish it before I leave.
Ito	Great. That would be very helpful. I'll see to it that you receive the necessary assignments right away.
Gabriella	Thank you.
Ito	As long as the budget is finished by tomorrow, then there shouldn't be a problem if <u>you're gone</u> during that time.

STEP 3 LANGUAGE DEVELOPMENT
1. working on
2. be an issue
3. approval to
4. final draft
5. As long as
6. am, willing to
7. be completed
8. take on extra work

REVIEW EXPRESSIONS
I 1. c   2. d   3. f   4. g   5. b   6. h   7. e   8. a
II 1. target   2. stable   3. concentrate
    4. approval   5. remain   6. fiscal year
    7. portion   8. assignment

CHAPTER 03 Sales

UNIT 01
STEP 2 LISTENING

Samantha	Now, there is <u>one last matter</u> I wish to discuss before we conclude our weekly sales meeting. This is going to be a very busy month for all of us. James, what's our goal?
James	We're aiming to <u>reach record sales</u> this month.
Samantha	Right. The reason we're anticipating this increase in business is the <u>buy-one-get-one-free</u> promotion we are offering in our branches.
Bruce	How long does it last?
James	The promotion will last <u>till the end of this month</u>.
Samantha	We need all of your customers to be aware that this offer lasts <u>only for a limited time</u>.
Bruce	What about the flyers? It could draw attention and give information about our promotion.
Samantha	Alright, let's give it a try! Please make sure to <u>give them out</u> to anyone that comes in to our branches.

STEP 3 LANGUAGE DEVELOPMENT
1. give it a try
2. record sales
3. buy-one-get-one-free
4. aim to
5. draw attention
6. for all of us
7. be aware
8. for a limited time

UNIT 02
STEP 2 LISTENING

Antonio	Hi, Monica, were you in today's staff meeting this morning? I wanted to attend, but I was with a client.
Monica	Yes, I was. The director <u>had a special announcement</u>. Our company finally acquired the renowned Japanese software company, Seiko Corporation.
Antonio	Is there any chance to be transferred to Japan? I <u>have been considering</u> working abroad for a long time.
Monica	Oh, really? Yes, you can apply. <u>Sooner or later</u> we will expand in the country.
Antonio	Well, it'd depend on the circumstances, but <u>I'm certainly open to</u> it.

Answer Key 123

Answer Key

HiEnglish

Monica	What about the language? You might need language training for the sales in Japan.
Antonio	I took Japanese classes in university for about three years.
Monica	That's great! Good luck!

STEP 3 LANGUAGE DEVELOPMENT

1. software company
2. was, open to
3. special announcement
4. apply
5. sooner or later
6. work abroad
7. for a long time
8. transfer to

REVIEW EXPRESSIONS

I 1. e 2. d 3. f 4. b 5. c 6. h 7. a 8. g

II 1. lasted 2. position 3. announcement
    4. flyers 5. record 6. renowned
    7. buy-one-get-one-free 8. sooner or later

CHAPTER 04 Advertising & Marketing

Unit 01

STEP 2 LISTENING

Carol	Is the advertising campaign for our new product coming along according to schedule?
Manuel	Yes, it is proceeding alright.
Carol	It is an important product of our company's this year, so we have to make sure to do a good job. Have you discussed the ad with the marketing team yet?
Manuel	Yes, and they're pleased with everything except for the background color. They've asked us to change it from dark blue to dark green.
Carol	Can we have it done on time?
Manuel	Once we've done that, it'll be ready to be sent to the print shop. We have plenty of time.
Carol	OK, but just keep in mind that we won't be able to send it out to them until next week. I heard that the print shop had to send out some printing equipment for repair, so they're backed up a bit.
Manuel	Oh, I'll check it out.

STEP 3 LANGUAGE DEVELOPMENT

1. plenty of
2. except for
3. come along
4. Keep in mind
5. According to
6. print shop
7. be pleased with
8. sent out

Unit 02

STEP 2 LISTENING

Gwen	So how was the second quarter's sales figure?
Alex	According to the sales report, our new product has not sold as well as we had anticipated.
Gwen	Why was there such poor performance?
Alex	After analyzing the data, we've come to the conclusion that we are not effectively reaching our target customer base for this product.
Gwen	What age group did you aim at?
Alex	Well, as we're talking about various accessories for electronic devices such as Bluetooth keyboards and speakers, we targeted consumers between 20 and 30 years old. But the sales are much lower than our projections.
Gwen	What about the marketing method? Is it still effective?
Alex	The marketing team still believes TV ads are the only way to show how detailed and delicate the products are, but I'm not convinced.

STEP 3 LANGUAGE DEVELOPMENT

1. target customer base
2. such as
3. come to a conclusion
4. sales figures
5. TV ads
6. sales report
7. aimed at
8. marketing method

REVIEW EXPRESSIONS

I 1. b 2. d 3. f 4. h 5. c 6. g 7. a 8. e

II 1. anticipate 2. advertising campaign
    3. Electronic devices 4. projections 5. repair
    6. According to 7. target customers 8. except

124 BUSINESS PIONEER 2

CHAPTER 05 Production & Manufacturing

UNIT 01

STEP 2 LISTENING

Tristan: The warehouse just called. They said they're still waiting to receive the last batch of a product. Is there something wrong with the production line at our plant?

Cecilia: Well, there seems to be a problem with the labeling machine because the product labels aren't sticking to the surface of the product. The technician is on his way to take a look at them.

Tristan: Did you report this to the warehouse manager?

Cecilia: Yes, I already informed him. He was concerned about making the deadline. How much has been produced so far?

Tristan: Actually, less than 70 percent.

Cecilia: It sounds like we should resume production as soon as possible.

Tristan: Right. Please give me a call with an update once you speak with the technician.

Cecilia: Sure, I will.

STEP 3 LANGUAGE DEVELOPMENT

1. on my way
2. be concerned about
3. make the deadline
4. sounds like
5. resume production
6. stick to
7. batches of
8. warehouse

UNIT 02

STEP 2 LISTENING

Russel: Good morning. Fast Export Company. How can I help you?

Jane: I'm afraid I have a serious complaint about your last delivery of products.

Russel: Oh, what's the problem? I hope the delivery arrived on time.

Jane: Yes, it was on time, but unfortunately the packaging was damaged.

Russel: Oh, I'm sorry to hear that. And the products?

Jane: I'm afraid a few items are defective. I know you would replace them if we sent them back, but it's getting close to the holidays, and we need the product urgently.

Russel: I understand. I'll pass on your complaints to the packaging department.

Jane: Sorry, but you really have to fix this for me today. It's extremely urgent. If it wasn't so urgent, I wouldn't call you, but we need the products now. I would be grateful if you sent the missing items immediately by express delivery.

STEP 3 LANGUAGE DEVELOPMENT

1. send, back
2. arrive on time
3. passed on
4. have a serious complaint
5. were damaged
6. would be grateful if
7. getting close
8. by express delivery

REVIEW EXPRESSIONS

I   1. d   2. e   3. f   4. g   5. b   6. c   7. h   8. a
II 1. immediately   2. complaints   3. delivery
    4. replaced   5. plant   6. informed
    7. resumed   8. warehouse

CHAPTER 06 Quality Control

UNIT 01

STEP 2 LISTENING

Vicky: During our last discussion, Mr. Kwan wanted us to visit him and examine the equipment. Is the defect rate still at 10%?

Jasmine: Yes. He suggested that actions should be taken to improve the manufacturing process.

Vicky: Have you looked at it, Michael? What's the problem?

Michael: Since Mr. Kwan's plant has several product lines, our specialist recommends that we inspect every one. We can locate the problem within a few days, but the factory will have to shut down during that time.

Vicky: Do you think we can make the deadline if we put off operations for a week?

Michael: Yes. Some employees can work over the weekend.

Jasmine: I'll let the managers know and find out how many employees can work overtime. If we don't have enough volunteers, we need to hire some temporary employees.

STEP 3 LANGUAGE DEVELOPMENT

1. manufacturing process
2. make the deadline
3. put off
4. work overtime
5. hires some temporary employees
6. shut down
7. product line
8. inspect every one

Answer Key

HiEnglish

UNIT 02
STEP 2 LISTENING

Carol I just came back from the assembly line, and <u>there seems to be</u> something wrong with the case for our product. It is too thick.

Kevin That's not good. I also noticed yesterday that the exterior finishing of our final product wasn't as thin and even <u>as it normally is</u>.

Carol The problem needs to be figured out quickly.

Kevin I wonder <u>what's causing the problem</u>. Do you think it might be molding?

Carol Hmm … That machine is very old, and it was repaired <u>quite a few times</u>. Maybe it's finally time to buy a new one.

Kevin As you know, we have to <u>get the director's approval for</u> the purchase, so I'll talk to him about it.

Carol When can I know? I need to inform the other managers of this issue.

Kevin I'll call you in the afternoon and confirm if <u>my request has been approved</u>.

STEP 3 LANGUAGE DEVELOPMENT
1. caused the problem
2. get, approval
3. It's, time
4. assembly line
5. come back from
6. figure out
7. quite a few times
8. inform, of

REVIEW EXPRESSIONS
I 1. e 2. d 3. h 4. a 5. f 6. c 7. b 8. g
II 1. operations 2. inspect 3. defective
    4. assembly line 5. regarding 6. overtime
    7. approval 8. inform

CHAPTER 07 Materials

UNIT 01
STEP 2 LISTENING

Denis Hi, I'm calling to see if I could <u>get some information about</u> the special material made by your company. I'm working for a local production plant, HNC, and my work involves purchasing materials for our new product.

Ellen Well, all of our items are made with <u>recycled materials</u>. And we also make sure that no pollutants are produced in the manufacturing process.

Denis My manager would definitely <u>be impressed by</u> that. We are developing an eco-friendly product.

Ellen Yes, many firms are these days, so we have become popular <u>all over the country</u>.

Denis But it's hard to imagine that items made of recycled materials could come in many varieties. Do you have <u>a large selection of</u> styles?

Ellen As a matter of fact, we do. We offer a variety of sizes and colors, just like regular materials.

Denis Can I see some for myself?

Ellen Sure, I'll mail some brochures of <u>our steady sellers</u> to you. I'm sure you'll like them.

STEP 3 LANGUAGE DEVELOPMENT
1. eco-friendly
2. all over the country
3. been impressed by
4. As a matter of fact
5. work for
6. recycled materials
7. get information
8. am calling to

UNIT 02
STEP 2 LISTENING

Tiffany Hi, Sam. We're out of parts C6 and F78 for model 6527. Could you <u>have someone bring</u> them here?

Sam Actually, we ran out yesterday. I <u>placed an order</u>.

Tiffany When will they arrive? I need to let the managers of each product line know about this.

Sam The supplier called me this morning and said the shipment is <u>behind schedule</u>.

Tiffany The deadline is coming up fast.

Sam I know, and the supplier did assure me that it would be here by next week <u>at the latest</u>.

Tiffany Well, I hope it will be here by this week because I guaranteed the partners' delivery by next week.

126 BUSINESS PIONEER 2

Sam	I'm not sure the supplier can do that, but I'll talk to them.
Tiffany	Thank you. Please let me know as soon as the shipment arrives so I can get to it ASAP.

STEP 3 LANGUAGE DEVELOPMENT
1. product line   2. placing an order   3. at the latest
4. behind schedule   5. as soon as   6. let me know
7. run out   8. is out of

REVIEW EXPRESSIONS
I   1. c   2. g   3. e   4. a   5. f   6. b   7. d   8. h
II 1. seller   2. recycled   3. brochure   4. guarantee
    5. materials   6. request   7. suppliers 8. shipment

CHAPTER 08 Research & Development

UNIT 01
STEP 2 LISTENING

Emmett	The National IT Conference takes place in two weeks. Have you had time to review the software presentation I prepared? I've tried asking the other engineers in our department, but none of them were available.
Kelly	You mean the new training software you developed?
Emmett	Yes, the one for nurturing technical support engineers.
Kelly	Yes, I've seen it, and it seems every innovative. I especially liked the interactive activities, and I think it's great that the audience will be able to try out the software.
Emmett	Exactly. I'm sure they will all be impressed when they see how it works.
Kelly	There's just one thing, Emmett. Make sure to tell the conference organizers that you'll need at least fifteen laptops for the participants. Otherwise, you will be the only one using the software.
Emmett	Thank you for the reminder. I'll let them know in advance.

STEP 3 LANGUAGE DEVELOPMENT
1. how it works   2. impressed   3. none of
4. technical support   5. try out   6. take place
7. otherwise   8. at least

UNIT 02
STEP 2 LISTENING

Arius	So, Fiona, could you report the development status of your new product?
Fiona	Sure. For those who don't know me, I'm Fiona Baxter, and I work in the R&D department. We've been developing a new electric device that the company is planning to launch next quarter. At the moment, we are testing product performance.
Arius	In that case, can we invite the manager of the sales team to the next meeting in order to update them on the product's features? This will better prepare them for future sales presentations.
Fiona	Yes, I believe so.
Arius	Great. During that meeting, why don't we also discuss the optimum market price?
Fiona	I think that is a good idea. My only concern is that since the new product is more costly to produce than previous models, it'll be sold at a higher price.
Arius	Alright. The agenda for the next meeting will be price determination. Please check the product specifications and market research data before attending.

STEP 3 LANGUAGE DEVELOPMENT
1. product specifications   2. In order to
3. market price   4. test product performance
5. planning to launch   6. work in
7. the status of   8. be more costly

REVIEW EXPRESSIONS
I   1. d   2. e   3. f   4. b   5. c   6. g   7. h   8. a
II 1. engineer   2. audience   3. nurture
    4. participant   5. status   6. previous
    7. determination 8. optimum

CHAPTER 09 Technical Issues

UNIT 01
STEP 2 LISTENING

Tanya	Good morning, this is Tanya in the tech department. How can I help you?
Jeremy	Hello, this is Jeremy Alvarez calling from the customer service department. I can't access the Internet on my computer, and I've got to send out some important emails this morning.

Answer Key

HiEnglish

Tanya	Okay, I need to get your computer's serial number. It should be on a small silver sticker <u>on the side of</u> the unit.
Jeremy	<u>Hold on a second</u>. I'll take a look at it.
Tanya	Take your time. Once I have that ID number, I'll <u>put in a service order</u> and send a technician this afternoon.
Jeremy	I found it. It's 45129586. But would it be possible for the technician to come before noon? I have a team meeting around that time.
Tanya	I see. I'll check if <u>someone is available</u> before noon.

STEP 3 LANGUAGE DEVELOPMENT
1. before noon   2. is available   3. send a technician
4. serial number 5. sent out   6. can't access
7. on the side of 8. Hold on a second

Unit 02
STEP 2 LISTENING

Janice	Ryan, how is the new software that we <u>recently installed</u> to track our merchandise inventory?
Ryan	Well, to be honest, it's not very useful. Since the software updates every 36 hours, it doesn't provide the most recent information.
Janice	Oh, I see the problem. When a customer checks <u>the availability of</u> an item, the inventory may show that the item is <u>in stock</u>, when in fact it's sold out.
Ryan	Hmm … There must be a way to adjust the update frequency. I'm going to check the settings to <u>see if it's possible</u> for the inventory to be updated every 24 hours.
Janice	Make sure each item is listed only once when updating information in the system. I'd like to avoid duplicate records in the database.
Ryan	Oh, I didn't know that. Thanks for letting me know.
Janice	If you're still <u>experiencing difficulties</u>, please call our team for assistance.

STEP 3 LANGUAGE DEVELOPMENT
1. update frequency   2. In fact   3. Since
4. To be honest   5. is, sold out   6. The availability of
7. experience difficulties   8. if it's possible

REVIEW EXPRESSIONS
I   1. g 2. f 3. a 4. h 5. b 6. e 7. d 8. c
II 1. merchandise   2. access   3. availability
    4. serial number 5. assistance 6. adjust
    7. technicians   8. noon

CHAPTER 10 Review

LISTENING
1. D
A.
A Ashely, what's our goal?
B We're aiming to reach record sales this month.
B.
A I took Japanese classes in university for about three years.
B That's great! Good luck!
C.
A Have you discussed the ad with the marketing team yet?
B Yes, and they're pleased with everything except for the background color.
D.
A Hi, Angela. We're out of parts C6 and F78 for model 6527. Could you have someone bring them here?
B Actually, we ran out yesterday, so I placed an order.

2. A
A.
A So how was the second quarter's sales figure?
B According to the sales report, our new product has not sold as well as we had anticipated.
B.
A Hi, Dean, were you in today's staff meeting this morning? I would like to have attended, but I was with a client.

B Yes, I was. The director had a special announcement.
C.
A Did you report this to the warehouse manager?
B Yes, I already informed him. He was concerned about making the deadline.
D.
A Hi, my name is Cynthia. I'm calling from Red Speed Logistics about the package under inspection.
B Oh, hi. I was about to call you.

READING
1. C   2. A   3. D   4. B   5. C

CHAPTER 11 Company

UNIT 01
STEP 2 LISTENING

Sylvia Congratulations! You've <u>been promoted</u> again!
Ryan Thank you so much!
Sylvia By the way, can you tell me about your company? I've heard of it, but I don't <u>know much about</u> it.
Ryan My company is the <u>world's fourth largest</u> automobile producer. It started in 1967 in Seoul, South Korea.
Sylvia It has been around for a long time.
Ryan <u>At the inception of</u> its foundation, the corporation was very small. Today, we sell vehicles in 193 different countries. And we have about 75,000 employees worldwide.
Sylvia What about <u>the revenue size</u>? It sounds pretty big.
Ryan Right. Its revenue is about 76 billion US dollars every year.

STEP 3 LANGUAGE DEVELOPMENT
1. the world's, largest   2. around for a long time
3. revenue size   4. automobile producer
5. been promoted   6. selling vehicles
7. in, different countries 8. the inception of

UNIT 02
STEP 2 LISTENING

Yolanda Hi, Roy. I wasn't expecting you to be here so early. I thought <u>you're scheduled to</u> work in the afternoon.
Roy Well, for the time being, I'll be working the morning shift. The manager <u>got transferred to</u> another building, so I'm <u>covering for</u> him until our team hires another person.
Yolanda Really? There's a manager position available on your team? I've been waiting for this kind of opportunity. Do you think I can still <u>submit an application</u>?
Roy Sure, but just be aware that you'll be working with many sub-groups.
Yolanda What do you mean?
Roy Well, for example, the Public Relations Team works with ours as a sub-group. If you're okay with that, you'd be <u>a good fit</u>.
Yolanda Thank you for the helpful information.
Roy You should hurry though. Interviews start next Monday.

STEP 3 LANGUAGE DEVELOPMENT
1. a good fit   2. submit an application
3. the morning shift   4. got transferred
5. work with   6. for the time being
7. is scheduled to   8. cover for

REVIEW EXPRESSIONS
I   1. f   2. e   3. d   4. a   5. g   6. b   7. c   8. h
II 1. revenue   2. shift   3. promoted
    4. expecting 5. inception 6. application
    7. foundation 8. scheduled

CHAPTER 12 Careers & Jobs

UNIT 01
STEP 2 LISTENING

Tim Hello, do you need any help? Are <u>you looking for</u> something?
Jackie Oh, I'm just waiting for the elevator.
Tim Do you work here?
Jackie Yes. My name is Jackie Hwang. I work on video games in the digital design team. I just <u>joined a month ago</u>.
Tim Oh, that's why! My name is Tim Tran. I work in marketing.
Jackie <u>How long have you worked</u> here?
Tim Almost five years. But when <u>I was first hired</u>, I was on the product team. One year later, I requested to transfer to the marketing team. There are many <u>opportunities for transferring</u> between teams at this company.
Jackie Thanks for the information.

Answer Key

HiEnglish

STEP 3 LANGUAGE DEVELOPMENT
1. Look for
2. opportunities for
3. How long have you
4. request to transfer
5. That's why
6. work in marketing
7. were hired
8. a video game designer

Unit 02
STEP 2 LISTENING

Russel — Hi, Martha. How is your project going? You've just started, right?

Martha — Right. I'm just waiting for the replies to your online survey about the recent changes to our website.

Russel — Really? John told me that they've already received them. I heard it was mostly positive feedback.

Martha — Did he? I need to check with him to make sure.

Russel — They especially liked the interactive features.

Martha — That's good, but I think we should add more questions to get more detailed information.

Russel — Alright. Do you have any suggestions?

Martha — Absolutely! I'll get back to you before I leave work today.

STEP 3 LANGUAGE DEVELOPMENT
1. positive feedback
2. How is, going
3. leave work
4. interactive features
5. online survey
6. detailed information
7. get back to
8. any suggestions

REVIEW EXPRESSIONS
I 1. e 2. a 3. g 4. c 5. h 6. d 7. f 8. b
II 1. marketing 2. employee 3. additional
   4. hired 5. replies 6. video game designer
   7. survey 8. interactive

CHAPTER 13 Colleagues

Unit 01
STEP 2 LISTENING

Gerald — How is work going so far, Sally? It's been about a month since you started.

Sally — Yes, right. I'm still getting used to it.

Gerald — What do you like best about your job?

Sally — Well, I like meeting people, and I enjoy talking to customers. What about you?

Gerald — My job's interesting, and I like working with the colleagues in my department. They're really nice.

Sally — I absolutely agree with you. But there has to be something you don't like.

Gerald — Well, I really dislike giving presentations. I'm always so nervous.

Sally — Yeah, me too.

Gerald — Well, I enjoyed talking, but I should get going. I promised to write a report, and I want to finish it today.

Sally — Okay. Gerald. I hope to see you at lunch again tomorrow.

STEP 3 LANGUAGE DEVELOPMENT
1. write a report 2. getting used to 3. so far
4. like working 5. agree with 6. It's been about
7. give presentations 8. enjoyed talking

Unit 02
STEP 2 LISTENING

Alana — Hi, Richard, how are you?

Richard — I'm doing well, how have you been doing?

Alana — Very good, thank you. Richard, I applied for transfer to another branch office because I had to move with my husband. So, Amanda, my colleague, will take over for me.

Amanda — Hi, nice to meet you.

Richard — Nice to meet you, too.

Alana — I already showed her records of your purchases.

Richard	Do you know when my contract needs to be renewed? Michelle always <u>notified me beforehand</u>.
Amanda	Sure, I was given all that information.
Richard	Great.
Amanda	Here's my card. If you have any questions, please <u>feel free to</u> let me know.

STEP 3 LANGUAGE DEVELOPMENT

1. take over
2. apply for
3. transfer to
4. Feel free to
5. branch office
6. do well
7. beforehand
8. records of purchases

REVIEW EXPRESSIONS

I 1. f 2. a 3. g 4. b 5. d 6. c 7. h 8. e
II 1. renew 2. record 3. colleague 4. report
   5. presentation 6. branch 7. department 8. apply

CHAPTER 14 Products

UNIT 01
STEP 2 LISTENING

Alison	Can you tell me about your latest tablet PC?
Russel	Yes, of course. You mean the Wide Edge? There are lots of great <u>new features in</u> the Wide Edge. It includes <u>an enormous amount of</u> storage and a super high speed processor.
Alison	What about the memory?
Russel	Well, <u>that depends on</u> the model. Wide Edge I has 64GB, and the Wide Edge II has 128GB. They are both <u>bigger than other common</u> tablet PCs.
Alison	That's true.
Russel	Old-fashioned tablet PCs had tiny screens, but the Wide Edge has a large 4K screen.
Alison	So, what does <u>this amazing device cost</u>?
Russel	This model, Wide Edge II, costs $99.
Alison	Well, I need to think about it. But thanks for the information.

STEP 3 LANGUAGE DEVELOPMENT

1. old-fashioned
2. tablet PC
3. need to think
4. depends on
5. bigger than
6. amount of
7. latest
8. new features

UNIT 02
STEP 2 LISTENING

Ben	I need someone to <u>translate</u> this contract and instructions <u>into Korean</u>.
Julia	Let's see … This is about one of our products, Wide Edge II.
Ben	Right. I need to send them to Korea <u>by next Monday</u>. Is there someone who can do this?
Julia	Well, as you know, most people in the global service team are on vacation. Peter <u>is on duty</u>, but I'm not sure if he can speak Korean.
Ben	If there is no one, we need to contact a translation service agency.
Julia	Okay. Do you need all parts to be translated? I think we can omit the audio translation function.
Ben	I don't think so. That is <u>one of the key features</u>. Frankly, our previous models were pretty bad.
Julia	Alright. I will ask Peter first <u>if he can handle</u> this and let you know.

STEP 3 LANGUAGE DEVELOPMENT

1. by next Monday
2. previous models
3. translate
4. on duty
5. on vacation
6. Frankly
7. am not sure if
8. As you know

REVIEW EXPRESSIONS

I 1. h 2. d 3. g 4. a 5. b 6. e 7. f 8. c
II 1. old-fashioned 2. latest 3. translate 4. duty
   5. omit 6. handle 7. devices 8. tablet

CHAPTER 15 Conflicts

UNIT 01
STEP 2 LISTENING

Eva	Ben, one of the production lines shut down <u>all of a sudden</u> and is not working now.
Ben	Again? We have to complete XNC's order <u>by next week</u>.
Eva	I'm worried that we won't be able to make enough supplies in time.
Ben	You're right. XNC is our biggest client. They don't appreciate delays.
Eva	So, this is not the first time this has happened? What did you do when the machine stopped working before?
Ben	Well, we turned it off, <u>let it cool down</u> for a while, and then we started it up again. Why don't you try that and <u>see if it works</u>?

Answer Key

HiEnglish

Eva I've already done that. I think we need to ask the technical support team to identify and <u>troubleshoot the problem</u>.
Ben Okay. I'll contact them myself.

STEP 3 LANGUAGE DEVELOPMENT
1. appreciate delays
2. all of a sudden
3. complete your order
4. shut down
5. turn off
6. stopped working
7. troubleshoot problems
8. cools down

UNIT 02
STEP 2 LISTENING
Scott What's wrong, Sandra? You look rather down.
Sandra My coworker, Carrie, is <u>getting me down</u>. She was friendly to me when I first joined the company, but now she's changed.
Scott Carrie? But she's a really nice person, and she <u>gets along well with</u> everyone. What has she done to upset you?
Sandra Well, she's really lazy, and I have to do all the work. She doesn't <u>take down phone messages</u>, and my customers get angry.
Scott Oh dear. That sounds bad.
Sandra The worst thing is she <u>tells stories about me</u> to the boss.
Scott Hmm, I think the best solution would be to talk to Carrie. If that doesn't help, you can always <u>ask for a transfer</u>.
Sandra Well, that's probably a good idea. I've got an appointment with human resources this afternoon. Keep your fingers crossed for me.

STEP 3 LANGUAGE DEVELOPMENT
1. take down
2. have got an appointment
3. get along well with
4. gets, down
5. joined the company
6. tell stories about
7. asking for a transfer
8. keep my fingers crossed

REVIEW EXPRESSIONS
I 1. d 2. f 3. b 4. g 5. h 6. c 7. a 8. e
II 1. troubleshoot 2. solution 3. upset

4. human resources department 5. delayed
6. tales 7. technical support team 8. sudden

CHAPTER 16 Collaboration & Cooperation

UNIT 01
STEP 2 LISTENING
Nick Okay, the visitors will arrive on Monday afternoon, and it's our job to take care of the Taiwanese group and <u>make them feel welcome</u>. Emily, have you reserved the hotel rooms yet?
Emily Yes, they're confirmed. I've already sent you the email.
Nick Good, thanks. Now on Monday evening we'll have dinner together. We'll <u>take everyone out</u> to a nice restaurant so that we can get to know each other. Any restaurant ideas?
Ashley I think we should take them somewhere where they serve <u>traditional Korean food</u>. Have you been to Hankook House, the new traditional Korean food restaurant in Bukchon Hanok Village yet?
Nick No, I've heard about it though. Isn't it expensive?
Ashley I haven't tried it either but I don't think it's too expensive. The food will be good, and the area is interesting for visitors, too.
Nick That sounds good. Could you check out <u>a couple of other places</u> too?
Ashley Will do.

STEP 3 LANGUAGE DEVELOPMENT
1. get to know
2. somewhere
3. feel welcome
4. take care of
5. has dinner together
6. a couple of
7. take, out to
8. traditional Korean food

UNIT 02
STEP 2 LISTENING
Jeffrey Good morning, Michelle. I submitted next year's budget request for my department, but I was wondering if you could <u>make a change</u>

	for me.
Michelle	Well, the deadline for requests was yesterday, but the financial director won't review them until tomorrow morning, so I should be able to help you.
Jeffrey	That's great. I want to replace the data software program in the list with a different one. It's a bit more expensive, but it will absolutely be more useful for my department's work.
Michelle	I've thought about your request, and since it's just one item, it won't be a problem.
Jeffrey	Thanks, I'm glad you approve it.
Michelle	Just let me know what the cost difference is, and I'll make the change now.
Jeffrey	Here is the final figure. Do you think I need to attach estimates?
Michelle	I think the director will definitely want to look at it.

STEP 3 LANGUAGE DEVELOPMENT

1. budget request
2. replace, with
3. I was wondering if
4. financial director
5. make changes
6. be a problem
7. The deadline for
8. final figure

REVIEW EXPRESSIONS

I 1. g   2. a   3. e   4. f   5. b   6. h   7. c   8. d
II 1. figure   2. estimate   3. welcomed
    4. traditional 5. confirm   6. district
    7. deadline   8. approve

CHAPTER 17 Culture

UNIT 01

STEP 2 LISTENING

Jessica	You're dressed quite casual. Haven't you been to work today?
Will	Yes, I have. This is our new office dress code. We don't have to wear formal clothes anymore.
Jessica	Why did your company change the dress code all of a sudden?
Will	We are keeping cooling costs down and saving energy by setting the air conditioner a little higher.
Jessica	And who came up with that idea?
Will	Ms. Martinez, my boss. She calculated the company's carbon footprint and was extremely shocked.
Jessica	I know about carbon footprints, but I've never checked mine. What was the result?
Will	It was huge. She says if we don't all become more environmentally friendly, we'll destroy the planet.

STEP 3 LANGUAGE DEVELOPMENT

1. save energy   2. office dress code
3. carbon footprint   4. come up with
5. environmentally friendly   6. destroy the planet
7. cooling costs   8. formal clothes

UNIT 02

STEP 2 LISTENING

Mia	Hi, Chen. Do you remember the business motto of our company? A board member asked me all of a sudden in a staff meeting, but my mind went blank.
Chen	Oh, you must have been so embarrassed. The motto is "Guts & Glory". I heard the founder wanted to motivate employees with this motto.
Mia	That's right! Why couldn't I remember such a short phrase?
Chen	I think it was introduced during the new employee orientation.
Mia	You're right! I remember now. That was a part of the required training.
Chen	This is why orientation is important. New employees get to learn about the company.
Mia	I absolutely agree! Remember Mr. Levinson's speech? All the new employees were inspired to work hard.

STEP 3 LANGUAGE DEVELOPMENT

1. required training   2. such a   3. was inspired to
4. new employee orientation   5. went blank
6. founder(s)   7. business motto   8. a part of

REVIEW EXPRESSIONS

I 1. c   2. e   3. a   4. g   5. f   6. b   7. h   8. d
II 1. carbon footprint   2. motto   3. calculate
    4. inspired   5. planet   6. dress code
    7. orientation   8. founder

Answer Key 133

HiEnglish

Answer Key

CHAPTER 18 Business Communication

UNIT 01
STEP 2 LISTENING

Alison   Hi, Joe. Are you attending the videoconference this afternoon?
Joe   I have to be there. I'm responsible for setting up the equipment, and I'm a bit nervous about it.
Alison   Oh? Why?
Joe   Remember the last time we had a videoconference? We had to stop because of technical issues.
Alison   Yes, I remember. I can see why you're nervous, but I'm sure it won't happen again.
Joe   Videoconferences are just so important for our work.
Alison   Of course. They're perfect for keeping in touch with our business partners.
Joe   Right. We have business contacts all over the world. We save time and transportation costs by videoconferencing.

STEP 3 LANGUAGE DEVELOPMENT
1. all over the world   2. am responsible for
3. set up the equipment   4. the last time
5. videoconference   6. business contacts
7. keep in touch with   8. technical issues

UNIT 02
STEP 2 LISTENING

Tanaka   Hi, Alison. Have you seen the website of Business World? There is an article that says we're the fastest growing mobile phone company in the country.
Alison   Oh, really? I haven't read it yet.
Tanaka   It's one of the top stories on their site.
Alison   Why don't you post a link to it on the company bulletin board?
Tanaka   Good idea. Media coverage will make employees feel pride in the company and what they do.
Alison   It will definitely help our recruiting campaign.
Tanaka   That's right! It will certainly attract more prospective job applicants to our company.
Alison   You'd better go off to your computer and add the link right now!

STEP 3 LANGUAGE DEVELOPMENT
1. go off   2. media coverage   3. post a link
4. Job applicants   5. the fastest growing
6. recruiting campain   7. one of the top stories
8. feel pride

REVIEW EXPRESSIONS
I   1. d   2. f   3. g   4. e   5. a   6. b   7. h   8. c
II   1. responsible   2. equipment   3. accommodations
     4. videoconference   5. prospective   6. coverage
     7. pride   8. recruiting

CHAPTER 19 Achievement

UNIT 01
STEP 2 LISTENING

Jess   Harry, I've got some great news. Jim Campbell, the program engineer, just told me that he can hold a workshop for our firm's employees the third week of this month.
Harry   That's good to hear. I understand that many companies want him as a programmer, so I'm happy that we were able to book him.
Jess   What should we do then?
Harry   We must verify the number of individuals attending so that we can make sure our room is large enough.
Jess   Should I send an email invitation to all employees?
Harry   Well, I guess you can email the department managers and ask them how many people will be going to the workshop.
Jess   That would be faster. I'll handle that.

STEP 3 LANGUAGE DEVELOPMENT
1. send an email invitation
2. hold a workshop
3. department managers
4. program engineer
5. be able to book
6. The number of
7. so that we can
8. large enough

UNIT 02
STEP 2 LISTENING

Tammy	Congratulations on your promotion, Ben. We'll certainly miss <u>having you on</u> the sales staff.
Ben	Thanks, Tammy.
Tammy	I know you'll be an excellent corporate trainer. I understand you've already prepared a series of training sessions on sales strategies.
Ben	That's right. I've been selling furniture for about ten years now in this store, and I have a lot of <u>effective sales methods</u> that I would like to share.
Tammy	What are some things you want to share?
Ben	You know, things like <u>establishing trust</u> with customers, communicating effectively, handling complaints, and so on.
Tammy	I've seen you <u>interacting with customers</u> many times. We can all <u>learn much from you</u>. When is your first session going to be?
Ben	In just three weeks, on July 21. I hope <u>you can make it</u>.

STEP 3 LANGUAGE DEVELOPMENT
1. handle complaints
2. in just three weeks
3. A series of
4. interacting with
5. training sessions
6. Congratulations on
7. establish trust
8. communicate effectively

REVIEW EXPRESSIONS
I 1. c 2. e 3. d 4. g 5. h 6. f 7. a 8. b
II 1. corporate trainer 2. complaints 3. workshop
   4. booked 5. verify 6. invitations
   7. strategies 8. promotion

CHAPTER 20 Review

LISTENING
1. B

A.
A I need someone to translate this contract and instructions into Korean.
B Let's see …. This is about one of our products, Wide Edge II.

B.
A Congratulations! You've been promoted again!
B Thank you so much!

C.
A Ben, one of the production lines shut down all of a sudden and is not working now.
B Again? We have to complete XNC's order by next week.

D.
A You look very casual. Haven't you been to work today?
B Yes, I have. This is our new office dress code. We don't have to wear formal clothes anymore.

2. C

A.
A I think we need to ask the technical support team to identify and troubleshoot problems.
B Okay. I'll contact them myself.

B.
A What's wrong, Sandra? You look rather down.
B My coworker, Carrie, is getting me down. She was friendly to me when I first joined the company, but now she's changed.

C.
A Hello, do you need help? Are you looking for something?
B Oh, I'm just waiting for the elevator.

D.
A Okay, the visitors will arrive on Monday afternoon, and it's our job to take care of the Taiwanese group and make them feel welcome.
B Yes, they're confirmed. I've already sent you the email.

READING
1. B   2. A   3. D   4. C   5. A

BUSINESS PIONEER Job English

지은이	윤주영
펴낸이	윤주영
펴낸곳	HiEnglish
펴낸날	2017년 2월 1일 초판 1쇄 발행
전화	(02) 335 1002
팩스	(02) 6499 0219
주소	서울 마포구 홍익로5안길 8
홈페이지	www.hienglish.com
이메일	editor1@hienglish.com
등록번호	제2005-000040호
ISBN	979-11-85342-25-2
Copyright	ⓒ 2017 HiEnglish
정가	16,000원
참여한 사람들	Sarah Kim, 한진, 정희정, Arius Derr, Ann Lowe

All rights reserved. No part of this publication may be reproduced, stored in a retrieval system, or transmitted in any form or by any means, electronic, mechanical, photocopying, recording, or otherwise, without the prior permission of the publisher.